Canoes and Kayaks
for the Backyard Builder

Skip Snaith

INTERNATIONAL MARINE
CAMDEN, MAINE

McGraw Hill

JAN 1 3 1994

This book is dedicated to the three captains: William Snaith, Fred Lawton, and Bucky Reardon, and to the ship that brought them together, *Figaro III*, and The Spirit of One in us all.

Acknowledgments to

Jonathan Eaton, for his vision and patience
Sherry and David Willmer, for being and seeing the light
Sherry Jagerson, for pure friendship
LJC, just because

Published by International Marine

10   9   8   7   6   5   4

Library of Congress Cataloging-in-Publication Data

Snaith, Skip
   Canoes and kayaks for the backyard builder.

   Bibliography: p.
   Includes index.
      1. Canoes and canoeing—Design and construction.
   2. Kayaks—Design and construction.   3. Boatbuilding.
   I. Title.
   VM353.S64   1988   623.8'29   88-8460
   ISBN   0-87742-242-7

Questions regarding the content of this book should be addressed to:
International Marine
P.O. Box 220, Camden, Me 04843

Typeset by Graphic Composition, Athens, GA; Printed and bound by Capital City Press, Montpelier, VT; Designed by Joyce Weston; Illustrations by Kelly Mulford; Cover photos by J. Michael Wyatt; Production by Janet Robbins; Edited by Jonathan Eaton, Jennifer Eliot, David Oppenheim

Contents

Preface

It has been said that the canoe (and by extension its cousin, the kayak) is the poor man's yacht. What other type of boat offers so much all-around utility, performance, and potential for exquisite shape and fine finish for so low an investment?

This book's instructions and drawings will enable almost anyone to build strong, shapely, lightweight canoes and kayaks using the taped-seam method. It's a boatbuilding technique that's ideal for first-time builders or those who might be frightened off by a high need for accuracy or specialized woodworking skills. In this technique, light plywood planks are cut to shape and bent into position on a simple building form. Their edges are joined together with fiberglass tape inside and out, making strong, waterproof joints. There's no need for the plank edges to fit perfectly to one another, since the tape and epoxy can bridge small gaps.

The canoe and kayak designs we'll build in the pages of this book are measured drawings, so no lofting is required before you start building. Plank shapes are given, so no lining off or spiling need fill your days with anguish or anxiety.

These taped-seam boats can be thought of as minimal in nature; they are defined more by what they don't have than by what they do have. You *can* build boats that don't need ribs, keels, stems, or sternposts. These canoe and kayak designs consist basically of planks, topped off by a rail and a deck where needed.

Defined by function, a boat is simply a contrivance that floats and is capable of carrying some kind of load over the water. Nowhere in its definition is implied or mentioned varnish, rabbets, keels, frames, hairline joints, copper rivets, cedar, oak, or any of the other articles of faith and holy relics that many people and publications would have you believe are part and parcel of the mystery.

The techniques and materials espoused in this book are fairly new, and there are still those who will look askance at them. But the laws of hydrodynamics will hold as true for your glued and taped canoe as they will for the most pristine original Rushton.

Even if your approach is functional to start with, it need not lack aesthetic appeal. Probably your first boat won't look like something that belongs in the North Shed at Mystic Seaport Museum, but you'll be out there paddling the thing. The next one is sure to look better. Best of all, you built it yourself!

I'll guide you step by step through building a canoe or kayak. We'll discuss design, setting up a shop, tools, finishing, and paddles. This book is intended as a guide to proven methods, but as in cooking (I wanted to call this *The Canoe and Kayak Cookbook,* but my publisher said no), familiarity with all recipes may lead the daring chef into variations on tried themes. After all, breathes there a boatman who doesn't feel that he can improve on his pet design, making it just a little more suited to his needs?

Taped-seam construction is a method that is well suited to experimentation and flexibility. Small changes in length, beam, or rocker are easily incorporated, and you can design as you build. The method is quick and inexpensive—a nice way to build a prototype and put those improvements to work.

Traditional builders changed mold spacing, keel or stem profiles, and whatever else they could to suit a customer's need, use available stock, or just to satisfy their own curiosity. You sometimes hear it said that they "never built the same boat twice."

Boats can be built in the "affix tab A into slot B" style, but in reality every step is an opportunity for choices. There isn't a single "best" wood to use for rails, and there isn't just one way to set up a boat or make a stem or put on a deck. Although I'll explain one sure way to put a boat together, I'll also offer you a choice of options and invite you to make an informed choice of your own.

There are as many ways to build as there are boats. I'll get you started with some quick and simple boats, but I hope you'll go on with some experimenting of your own. Keep your eyes open—and have fun!

1. Principles of Design

Boat design is both art and science. Calculation alone, without the tempering of experience, cannot be relied upon. If aesthetics are involved this becomes all the more true, for there is no formula for beauty.

Probably more canoes and kayaks have been built by eye or by rule of thumb than were ever "designed." But knowing what factors affect hull performance—even on a general level—can help you decide the overall parameters your boat should fit, or aid in analyzing why an existing boat acts the way it does in a given set of conditions.

The information in this chapter will give you some of the basics of design; an understanding of these principles isn't necessary if you simply want to follow the step-by-step building instructions later in the book, but it will greatly enhance your understanding of your boat's performance and your appreciation of other boats you'll come across in the future.

A listing of books that go into greater theoretical detail appears in Appendix A.

Length

This is everybody's favorite dimension. People are forever wishing that their boat were just a little longer or a little shorter.

There are two real advantages that come with length. First, the longer the boat, the higher its potential speed. In simple terms, a longer hull makes a larger wave as it goes through the water. Waves, being essentially large ripples, move at a known speed, which increases with their size. Thus, unless a boat skims above the waves, its speed is more or less limited to the speed of the wave it creates in front of itself.

Second, you can increase displacement (which translates into load-carrying ability) with the least effect on wetted surface (which leads to resistance) by increasing length.

Third, with everything else equal, you increase stability as you increase length.

Given these facts, you may wonder why people put up with short boats, but there are reasons for this, too. Shorter craft are much easier to handle, both in the water and out. In narrow creeks and tight corners the longer craft is at a disadvantage, as it can be for cartopping and in storage.

One of the distinct appeals of the canoe or kayak is that it can be a one-man boat, and if it is too long or heavy to be carried or launched alone it defeats that purpose.

1

Many people feel that tracking (or the ability to keep going in a straight line) depends on length. A truer answer would be that it does and it does not. A good hull shape above and below water is really the best way to ensure that your boat tracks well. I have personally seen a 10-foot Rushton out-track 15- to 17-foot kayaks in a following sea.

Beam

The beam, or width, of a boat obviously affects its stability. Beam and length are often expressed as a ratio, since beam is a relative concept. What is wide for a 12-footer would be narrow for a boat twice as long.

A boat's beam is measured at several horizontal planes through the hull. Two key locations are at the waterline and at the deck or sheerline. It's also important to know the point at which the maximum beam appears in a fore-and-aft plane. Maximum beam is not always located exactly amidships; in fact, the modern trend has been to move maximum

Figure 1-1. A sampling of profile shapes.

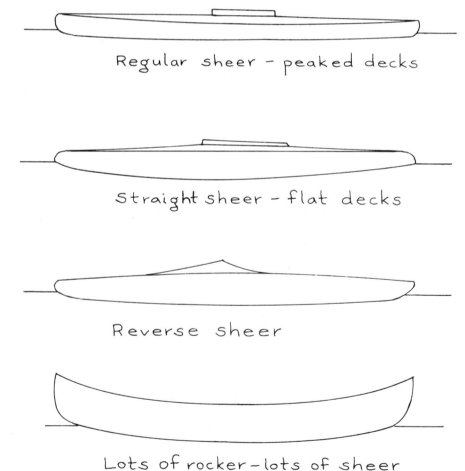

Regular sheer - peaked decks

Straight sheer - flat decks

Reverse sheer

Lots of rocker - lots of sheer

beam farther and farther aft in many boat types, canoes and kayaks included.

Width is an extremely important factor in stability, but width alone does not carry the same guarantee of stability at sea that it does on land. For instance, a wide, flat boat will have very high initial stability, but this vanishes quickly once a critical angle of heel is reached. This makes the boat susceptible to capsize by wave action. To compound the problem, the high initial stability can reassert itself once the boat is upside down, which can make righting, in the case of a kayak, difficult.

In paddle-powered craft excessive beam can make paddling uncomfortable and tiring, so it is to be carefully avoided. Tumblehome is a way of dealing with this problem. With tumblehome, the hull at the sheerline is narrower, while the maximum beam is much nearer the waterline. The theory is that the wide low part gives you the bearing you need, while the narrow upper part makes paddling easier. In racing boats this is exaggerated—due to racing rules—but it is seen in many open canoes as well.

Kleppers and Folboats, at about 32 inches wide, represent the outer range for kayaks. Some Greenland and Aleut skinboats, by contrast, were a mere 18 to 19 inches across. Most modern kayaks fall between 20 and 25 inches in width.

Canoes range from about 26 inches in width for a solo canoe up to 36 inches or better for a big guide canoe.

These numbers are for reference only, but remember that a modest increase in beam can rapidly magnify sectional area and wetted surface, leading to higher frictional coefficients and a slower, harder-to-drive hull.

Depth Amidships (Freeboard)

A good many modern boats (sail, power, oar, and paddle) are too high-sided. This excessive freeboard is thought to give more usable space, to keep the boat drier, and even to improve seaworthiness. But many times, especially in the last case, just the opposite effect results.

A high-sided canoe or kayak, or one with really swept-up ends, presents an unnecessarily large surface area, which makes maneuvering difficult and causes poor tracking in a crosswind.

While higher-sided craft may take on a bit less spray, susceptibility to windage may be too high a price to pay for a marginal increase in comfort.

In kayaks, because of the seating position, low freeboard allows interference-free paddling and lets you take your stroke with the paddle held lower. This means less strain, especially on a windy day.

The critical locations at which to measure hull depth are amidships and at the ends. In a good hull (one with lift and flare), a few inches of freeboard will keep you surprisingly dry in all but the nastiest chop.

Figure 1-2. An Arctic skinboat. (Yale Collection of Western Americana Beinecke Rare Book & Manuscript Library)

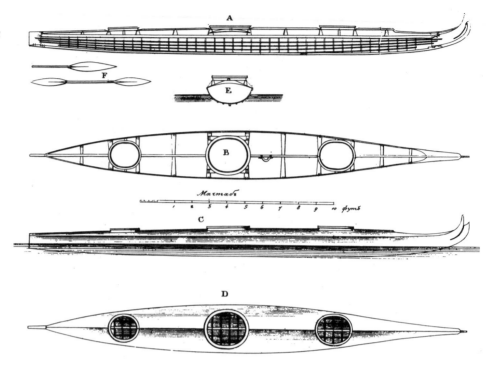

Clearly we are talking about a decked boat in this case, but even an open canoe will not require much more if it is a good model.

The normal sheerline associated with boats (especially sailboats and canoes) is low in the center and higher at the ends. This is not always appropriate in kayaks because they are so much lower on the water to begin with. The danger is that to get a good-looking conventional sheer, you will probably end up with too much windage in the ends. A flat or even reversed sheer can be the answer, and this solution is exemplified by several Arctic skinboat types, especially those intended for use on open water.

Lateral Plane

Lateral plane is related to depth but by no means irrevocably bound to it. It is that area of a boat's underwater shape that is designed to resist the natural tendency toward sideways motion through the water. A sailboat's keel is the most familiar example.

Because shallow draft is an advantage in canoes and kayaks, they generally lack extensive lateral plane. Since an external keel is generally a hindrance on these boats, they develop almost all their lateral plane via hull shape. The best and favorite tactic is to use sharp entry and exit lines, but the use of hollow waterlines, V-shaped sections, and chine construction can all do their part.

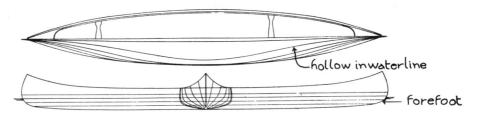

Figure 1-3. A sharp entry and exit, as seen in the plan view of the lines drawing for the Arkansaw Traveler, a "Canadian-model light paddling canoe" offered in the J. Henry Rushton catalog of 1903, keeps buoyancy out of the ends and results in a deep forefoot and afterbody as seen in the profile view, for good lateral plane. The effect is heightened by a pronounced hollow in the waterlines near the ends. See page 7 for more on waterlines.

The balance of lateral plane is as important as its amount. An unbalanced hull will tend to weathercock, and may be susceptible to broaching or being steered by wave action, especially when running or quartering (with the wind coming from behind at an angle). This tendency is even more apparent if the boat is surfing on the waves.

Rocker

Rocker is the amount of longitudinal curvature in the keel. Basically, the more rocker, the more maneuverable the boat becomes, spinning on the proverbial dime.

As a general rule for canoes and kayaks, 1 to 1½ inches is low to moderate, while 3 to 4 inches is a lot. Of course, it is necessary to look at rocker in light of the attitude or angle that the keel assumes when the boat is floating on her marks in the water. The keel may have drag, which means that it becomes progressively deeper over the run aft, and this can magnify or nullify the effect of rocker when judged as a whole.

Figure 1-4. A keel with moderate rocker, and a straight keel with drag. A canoe profile with pronounced rocker is shown in Figure 1-1.

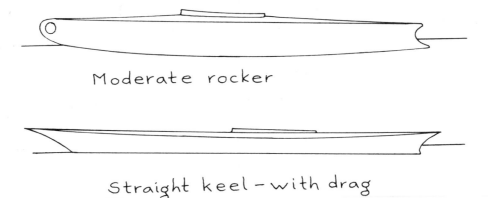

In general, a shorter boat can take more rocker and still be called "normal" than can a longer one of the same type. (This applies more to the difference between a 9-foot and a 12-foot boat than to that between a 20-foot and a 30-foot one.) In other words, really short boats generally like a little more rocker.

In touring kayaks (sea kayaks) there is a lot of emphasis on tracking, but this should not be achieved at the expense of maneuverability. Boats that are hard to course-correct or that don't respond easily with small attitude changes in a seaway are not performing as they should. It is my experience that tracking and maneuverability are not mutually exclusive traits.

Deadrise

Deadrise is the angle of the bottom planking in relation to the horizontal. The difference between a flat-bottomed boat and a V-bottomed one is that the latter has deadrise and the former doesn't.

Deadrise has long been associated with speed, seaworthiness, and sail-carrying ability (read stability), but excessive deadrise causes low initial stability and reduced hull volume. Deadrise can contribute to a boat's rough-water stability and may lessen any tendency to pound, while increasing lateral plane. Angles of roughly 10 to 15 degrees are usual in a 'midships section.

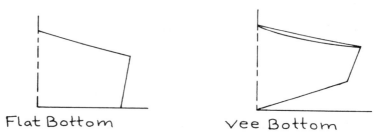

Flat Bottom   Vee Bottom

Figure 1-5. The 'midships sections of a flat-bottomed and a V-bottomed boat, as viewed from forward, port sides only. The deadrise (exaggerated in this rendition), greater lateral plane, and reduced hull volume of the latter are apparent.

Entries and Exits

In order for a boat—or a story—to be any good it needs a beginning, a middle, and an end. In terms of laminar flow (the molecular layer of water flowing immediately against the hull), the bow is the beginning and the stern is the end. The middle is anywhere in between.

The ideal beginning or entry is like a surgeon's knife, clean and quick to get things started. The middle, like the plot, is expected to carry it

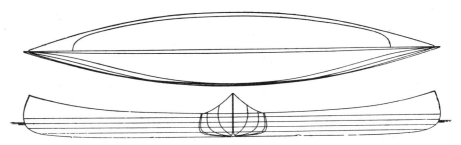

Figure 1-6. Sharp, hollow waterlines in the ends of this hull's underbody, combined with fuller waterline ends topside, produce a sharp entry and exit with adequate reserve buoyancy and stability. Note the generous lateral plane in the profile view. This is the Igo, another "Canadian model" canoe from the 1903 Rushton catalog.

along with no dragging until it all gets neatly wrapped up at the end, or stern, with a minimum of confusion and turmoil.

Creating these fine ends is not as simple as it seems, for with fineness comes a lack of buoyancy, which encourages them to plunge or dive into the waves. The trick is to use flare or hollow to create wider sections above the waterline. These wider sections are not normally immersed and do not add to wetted surface except when required to increase buoyancy, stability, or both. A boat so designed will not drag a lot of water around after her and should make a minimal wake.

Do not think of the entry or exit in connection with the bow and stern alone, since the waterlines, the sections, and the run are all involved. They are best conceived of as the synthesis of several features. In a canoe or kayak the entry and exit are the best chance to get good lateral plane, and as a consequence they had better be good.

Waterlines and Sections

Waterlines and sections are the major components by which a lines drawing of a boat is made. Together, they go a long way toward describing her shape.

Waterlines are horizontal planes parallel to the water's surface. Sections are vertical planes perpendicular to the boat's centerline. In a nongeometric analogy, waterlines are like pieces of bread in a multilayer sandwich lying on a plate. Sections are like the slices in a loaf of bread as it rests on a shelf.

The primary waterline considered is the load waterline (LWL). This is the line the boat floats on with her normal crew and gear aboard. For design purposes, other waterlines are drawn above and below that one and parallel to it.

There is no single most important section, but usually the 'midships

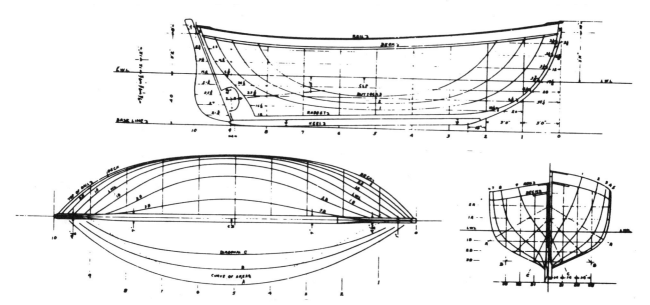

Figure 1-7. The lines of a Tahiti ketch, designed by John Hanna. Studying the waterlines and buttock lines can give you a sense for how cleanly a hull will slide through the water. In this hull the ends are pinched; note the tight radii of the underbody waterlines in the ends, and note too that the buttock lines (longitudinal slices through the hull at incremental distances from the boat's centerline) are fairly closely spaced below the load waterline in profile view. The designer's art has faired these curves into a pleasing form, and Tahiti ketches have sailed the world's oceans safely and comfortably, but this hull will drag water with it rather than shedding water cleanly as it passes by, and is an obvious example of characteristics which work for another type of boat but are inappropriate for a canoe or kayak hull. (Reproduced from A Ketch Called Tahiti: John G. Hanna and His Yacht Designs, *by Stephen Doherty, IMP, 1987)*

section and a few of the forward and after sections are needed to give an indication of general hull shape.

It is important to realize that the waterlines and sections are not separate entities but parts of a whole—with each curve flowing into the next. Also, sections and waterlines are dependent on one another. They are really different views of the same thing—a point, or a series of points, on the hull in question.

Waterlines show the distribution of displacement throughout the boat, and are important clues as to her probable stability and performance.

Waterlines also indicate a lot about the type of entry or exit of a hull. Taken in conjunction with the buttock lines, they can give a good idea of the laminar flow that the hull exhibits. Obviously, you want a smooth, clean flow with few or no eddies, because turbulence causes drag. Put another way, it means that more energy is needed to move the boat. Waterlines with sudden turns or tight radii generally indicate that water flowing past them will need to take tight turns as well. And that's what turbulence is all about.

Sectional shape can vary from flat-bottomed to V to round. Sections give an indication of stability, bearing (resistance to heeling forces), and hull volume at a given point. Generally, flat and shallow-V sections will have high initial stability, as discussed earlier under beam. The deep Vs and round bottoms may have a somewhat lower initial stability, but stability usually increases as the angle of heel grows larger, and ultimately these shapes may be more stable.

There are really no hard and fast rules, and good and bad examples exist of each type. Personal prejudice and levels of ability and familiarity also play a large role in a person's judgment of a given boat or a type, and comparison and study comprise the only way to see which shapes work, and which don't, for you.

Figure 1-8. Two round-bottomed hulls, showing slack versus hard bilges. Flat- and V-bottomed sections are shown in Figure 1-5.

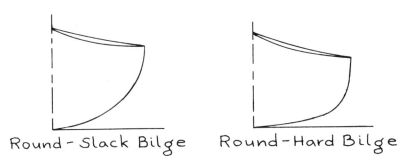

Round – Slack Bilge   Round – Hard Bilge

The Run

The run is the underwater afterbody of the hull, beginning either where the keel commences to curve upward toward the surface or, lacking this, aft of the section of greatest area. The run is important since it is the path the water takes as it is released by the hull. An easy, almost straight line with no sudden kinks is often best, but again, there is no single rule. The parting of the hull and the laminar flow should be as gentle as possible, because waves and turbulence here will hold the boat back significantly.

A bad run and stern will largely undo any good design forward, so its importance is not to be underestimated.

Wetted Surface

The sum total of your boat's underwater area is her wetted surface. In low-powered hulls like canoes and kayaks, the drag created by this area is the main limitation of speed and the main drain of power.

The distribution of this area is important. For instance, due to friction the laminar flow is fastest at the bow and slowest at the stern. Logic indicates, then, that a boat can better tolerate area aft where the effects of friction will be lessened. This is the classic argument for the fine bow and increased bearing aft that modern Swedeform hulls exhibit.

The attempt to cut wetted surface leads to fine underwater lines, which in turn can have a negative effect on stability, so for any given boat a balance will need to be struck.

Hull Volume

Volume is related to the displacement capabilities of a given hull, and also to its interior space.

In canoes, the decision on volume really depends on how much load you wish to carry. But the type of canoeing being undertaken will influence this factor to a degree. A whitewater canoe will have more volume and thus more reserve buoyancy than a racing boat, in reflection of its specific needs.

In kayaks, the matter of volume is closer to the bone since there is less to go around. In whitewater, use of more volume means more flotation, but the current trend among slalom boaters, hot-doggers, and freestylists is for less and less volume. In touring or sea kayaks, the trend is toward high-volume boats, for better or worse. High volume means high load-carrying capacity, lots of interior space, and high-peaked, water-shedding decks. It can also mean a heavy boat, a lot of windage, and a craft that doesn't paddle well without being weighted down. There is a thin line between a big, comfortable boat and something that you rattle around in like an empty house.

Lower-volume boats can offer a tight fit that promotes a oneness of boat and paddler. They can be quite light and responsive, free from the worst effects of windage that make rudders and skegs mandatory for so many of today's kayak designs. They can be a lot more fun on day or weekend trips, but the choice is a personal one, based on the type of paddling you do.

Weight

Weight is a critical factor that is often overlooked. Human power is low power, somewhere around ¼ h.p. for a sustained period. Excess weight robs you of power, which translates into speed or distance.

Almost all of today's canoes and kayaks are too heavy, in my opinion. It is still popular to claim an Eskimo design heritage, but many of these boats weigh two to four times as much as the originals. This is a hefty discrepancy in anybody's book.

Beyond the ability to dampen response times or quickness of motion, weight does little to add to a boat's seaworthiness or stability. It is an old truism that a nimble boat is a good seaboat, even if it is not always the most comfortable.

You can paddle farther faster in a light boat, which means less exposure on long trips and crossings. You can carry more gear in the same space, since your duffle is a greater percentage of the boat's displacement. Finally, putting in and taking out, as well as the whole cartopping problem, is significantly eased.

Weight saving is one area where the wooden boat shines, because wood is inherently lighter and stiffer than the composites, with excellent strength and elasticity.

A Summation

I'd love to come up with an overall summation of canoe design—and it might be comforting to read such a distillation of knowledge. Unfortunately, it would stand a good chance of being wrong or misleading.

A given boat is a synthesis of many different lines, shapes, and features. It's tempting to think that one feature—a prominent type of bow, sheer, or rocker, for instance—may be the key to understanding the boat's particular nature, but it would be unwise to forget the rest of the boat. A sharp bow may well be supported by a certain degree of flare, or hollowness in the waterlines, and perhaps a generous sectional area farther aft which is less noticeable but essential.

It is difficult to determine how one part of the hull flows into another, where the boundaries are, and how the differing aspects affect one another. The boat is a whole and must be approached as such.

Designs should be looked at in light of their intended function, constructional and material considerations or limitations, economic factors, and the actual conditions of use. Do not confuse considerations arising from economic needs with hydrodynamic ones, and be sure you understand which needs took priority in the creation of a given design. The generous beam in one man's solo canoe may reflect nothing more than the owner's refusal to be separated from a particular cooler while on the water.

Mistakes, your own or those of others, may be as enlightening or more so than successes. It is often easier to tell why a boat doesn't work than to sort through the subtle interrelations that make up a really successful boat. Often a bad boat is the best teacher.

Study and comparison on the water is the surest way to make meaningful distinctions between designs. Absorption through exposure and use will lead to useful knowledge and give flesh to the bones of theory. A study of the best efforts from the past is the strongest foundation for tomorrow's successes.

2. The 11-foot Taped Canoe

This is a solo canoe, transportation for one person on waters varying from creeks and swamps to lakes and salt water. She needs to be an able boat, decently stable, at home in a sea or a crosswind. At the same time, she needs to be lightweight, responsive, pretty to look at, and fun to paddle. How does this particular boat measure up?

Rushton's famous Wee Lassie is our touchstone for comparison purposes. The Lassie is a classic, round-bottomed hull. Her bilges are "slack," in that there is no discernible point where the curve of the hull takes any radical turns or changes direction more quickly than in another spot. This produces a stability that is initially low, but quickly rises as the angle of heel increases, mostly because the immersed area of the hull cross section increases rapidly as she goes over.

The 11-foot taped canoe is a compromise in that we are using four planks where Rushton used seven or so. This gives her a more chined look and a more pronounced deadrise to her bottom. But in spite of that, there is no "chine" feel to the boat, no lurch or "pop" or sharp transition in the stability as you lay her over onto her side; she picks up stability the farther over she goes. There isn't a constant flare in her midsection and her sheer plank is almost dead vertical; she doesn't need flare to keep her stable.

Most of the work in designing this boat lay in picking the width and angle of each of the planks so that even though she is made up of discrete angles, the overall effect is as close to a round-bottomed shape as possible. The angle of the garboard (deadrise) and the next plank in the "turn" of the bilge are particularly important in controlling the shape. The deadrise in her bottom is almost the maximum amount without making her a more cranky, low-initial-stability hull. In comparison the Rushton has a flatter bottom and an easier transition from horizontal to vertical planking orientation.

Like the Rushton, this 11-footer has very sharp ends that flare easily as they approach the sheer. She also has some hollow in her waterlines, though not as much as could be worked in with more planks. The effect of all this is to give her bite on the water for tracking, and to let her cut cleanly into oncoming waves. At the same time, the flare and the hollow give her lift to keep her from burying her nose.

The keel rocker is balanced evenly fore and aft, but there's only about 1½ inches of rocker. She's not a freestyler that will spin on a dime and do tricks for the paddler, but putting more rocker in her keel (at least another inch) and changing the profile of the stem and stern (especially where they meet the bottom, to be more cut away) would probably accomplish this. Were I to change anything with the boat, I would probably

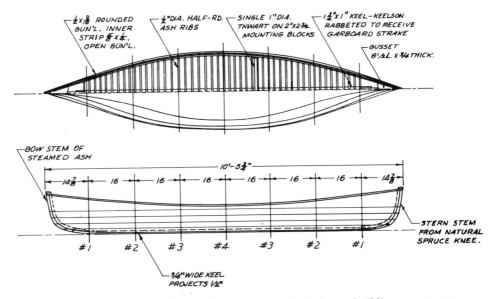

Labels on upper drawing:
⅛ x ⅞ ROUNDED GUN'L. INNER STRIP ⅝ x ¼. OPEN GUN'L.
½" DIA. HALF-RD. ASH RIBS
SINGLE 1" DIA. THWART ON 2" x 2¾ MOUNTING BLOCKS
1¾" x 1" KEEL–KEELSON RABBETED TO RECEIVE GARBOARD STRAKE
GUSSET 8½" L. x ¾ THICK.

Labels on lower drawing:
BOW STEM OF STEAMED ASH
10'-5¾"
14⅞ — 16 — 16 — 16 — 16 — 16 — 16 — 14⅞
STERN STEM FROM NATURAL SPRUCE KNEE.
#1 #2 #3 #4 #3 #2 #1
¾" WIDE KEEL PROJECTS ½"

Figure 2-1. John Henry Rushton, of Canton, New York, began building canoes more than a century ago. His many models, including the Ugo, Indian Girl, and Arkansaw Traveler, have been much admired and coveted for their lapstrake cedar planking, light weight, and fine craftsmanship. The Wee Lassie, pictured above, was the inspiration for the 11-foot taped canoe in this book. (Reproduced from Rushton and His Times in American Canoeing, *by Atwood Manley,* The Adirondack Museum/ Syracuse University Press, 1968)

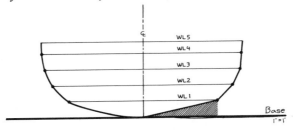

Figure 2-2. Wee Lassie's midsection with its original round bilge (left) and in a five-plank taped-seam adaptation (right). The taped-seam version incurs a few compromises, but these are not pronounced.

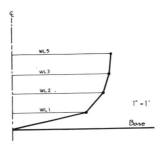

Figure 2-3. Reducing the number of planks in the taped-seam version from five to four can be accomplished with minimal disruption of the boat's best characteristics by changing the control points very slightly—specifically, by moving the points at waterlines 2 and 3 in Figure 2-2 up and out, and ignoring what was waterline 4.

Figure 2-4. The 11-foot by 27-inch solo canoe. Two tables of offsets are shown. The first gives heights above the base shown in the profile drawing—in other words, the standard presentation. The second table is included for your convenience in building the boat upside down, and gives heights above the baseline established by the top of your strongback (see Chapter 7).

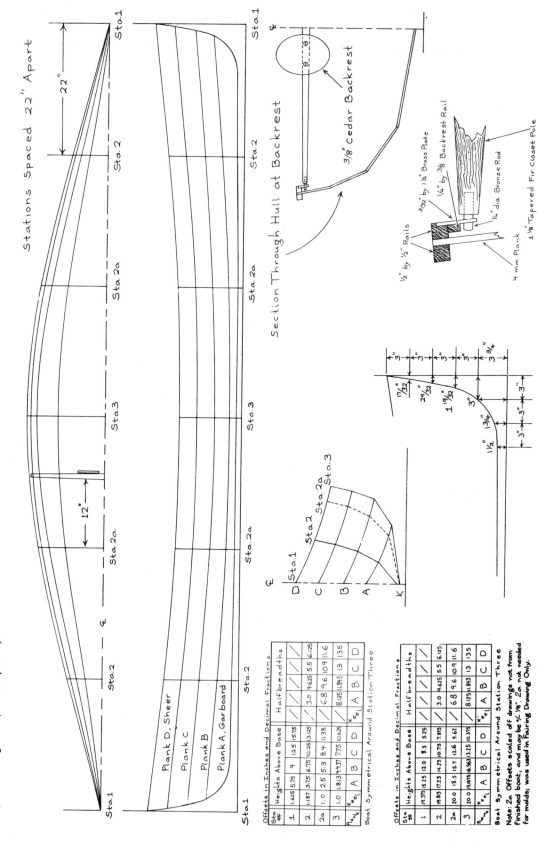

Offsets in Inches and Decimal Fractions

Sta #	Heights Above Base keel	A	B	C	D	Halfbreadths keel	A	B	C	D
1	1.625	5.75	9	12.5	15.75	/	3.0	4.625	5.5	6.125
2	1.187	3.75	6.75	10.25	13.125	/	6.8	9.6	10.9	11.6
2a	1.0	2.5	5.3	8.4	11.38	/	8.125	11.843	13	13.5
3	1.0	1.813	4.437	7.75	10.625	/			13	13.5

Boat Symmetrical Around Station Three

Offsets in Inches and Decimal Fractions

Sta #	Heights Above Base keel	A	B	C	D	Halfbreadths keel	A	B	C	D
1	14.375	15.75	12.0	8.5	5.25	/	3.0	4.625	5.5	6.125
2	14.813	17.25	14.25	10.75	7.875	/	6.8	9.6	10.9	11.6
2a	20.0	18.5	15.7	12.6	9.62	/	8.125	11.843	13	13.5
3	20.0	19.0875	16.563	13.25	10.375	/			13	13.5

Boat Symmetrical Around Station Three

Note: 2a Offsets scaled off drawings not from finished boat, and may be ±1/8". 2a not needed for molds; was used in Fairing Drawing Only.

Figure 2-5. Measured plank drawings for the 11-foot canoe. If your molds were to come out exactly as mine did, you could replicate these plank shapes with complete assurance that they would fit together as designed. In fact, however, some minor variability from one set of molds to the next is virtually inevitable, so I recommend that you do the final fitting of the planks as described in Chapter 10.

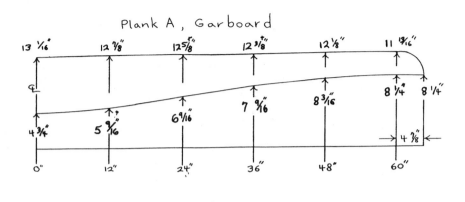

Plank A, Garboard

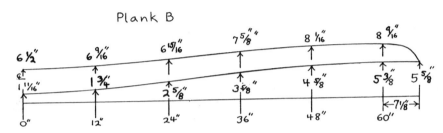

Plank B

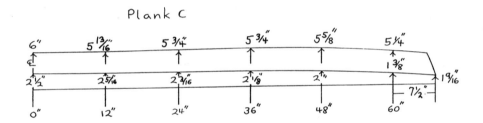

Plank C

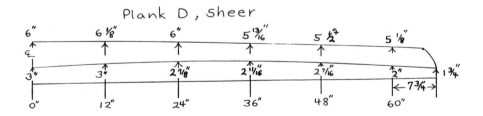

Plank D, Sheer

change the profiles to get just a tad bit more maneuverability without compromising her excellent tracking.

Her freeboard is low; she's less than a foot deep amidships, but there is enough rise in the ends to keep her pretty dry and safe in a tumble. Her ability to rise to waves is an important factor in deciding how deep she should be.

Figure 2-6. A Wee Lassie and a taped-seam adaptation side by side, showing their sharp ends and the gentle flare in their bow sections.

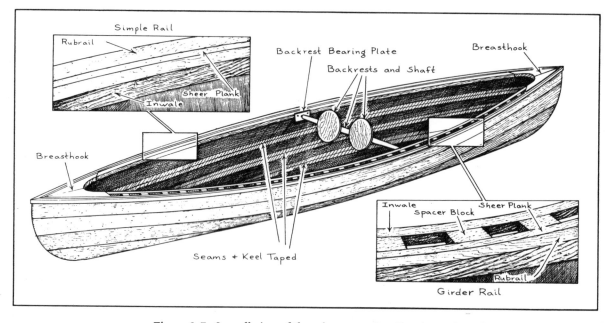

Figure 2-7. Overall view of the solo canoe, showing the option of a solid versus a girder-type rail, as discussed in Chapter 11.

Her 27-inch beam is pretty standard for a boat of this type. It's wide enough to feel comfortable, but not a detriment to paddling.

The hull is light enough so that the lone paddler can cartop it with ease or pack it into a distant pond. This kind of versatility has to be experienced to be appreciated. Before glassing, the hull weighs under 20 pounds; with glassing and all woodwork complete, she should weigh about 25 to 27 pounds—maybe even less.

All in all I am quite pleased with this boat. She offers a lot of performance for a minimum number of planks, and is one of the simplest packages you might find.

3. The 16-foot Sea Kayak

T he challenge in this design was to make a three-plank boat, but not to have the design ruled by the simplicity of the hull. (Three planks are not a lot of material to work with.) Most of my inspiration came from the skinboats of the Arctic, many of which are V-bottomed, chined hulls. The flexibility of the skin covering offers some subtleties that plywood is less able to render—at least in large sheets.

The boat has a strongly veed midsection with a fair amount of deadrise carried out into the ends. There is a small amount of continuous flare above that, right to the sheer. The garboard and the plank above it form a strong chine. For all but the heavier paddlers (especially in an unloaded condition), she will tend to float on this narrow vee section, with the result that her initial stability will be low (somewhat along the lines of a Nordkap or similar hull). Stability increases as the boat heels, but less experienced paddlers may be uncomfortable with this characteristic.

With a payload she will float lower, gaining more immersed section. Paddlers can carry water ballast to achieve this if they are otherwise unloaded.

Almost all her length overall is waterline length, and she moves quickly through the water with little fuss and a good turn of speed for her size. The long straight keel makes her track well—she is no slalom boat!

The sheer is flat, which is a good way of balancing windage while avoiding high ends. This is consistent with her skinboat heritage.

A peaked deck complements the large volume of the hull, offering room for gear and your knees as well. She is 17 inches deep from keel to cockpit rim. Less expeditionary-minded paddlers could lower the height of the deck beams or put on a flat deck with my blessing.

The cockpit is bigger than I usually make, but it is comfortable and of a more or less standard size for today's boats. I chose a flat laminated rim as the easiest to make, and suited to the deck's 3-inch pitch.

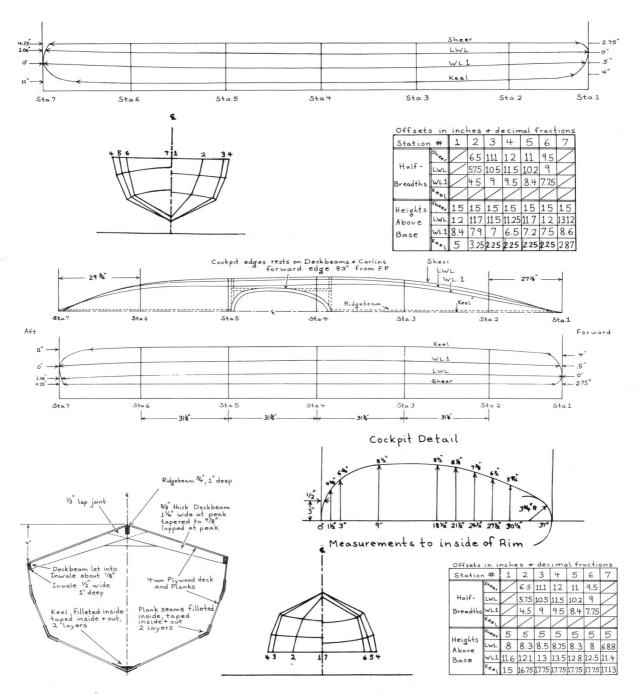

Figure 3-1. Lines drawing of the 16-foot sea kayak we'll build in the pages of this book. The inspiration for this boat was the skinboats of the Arctic (see Figure 1-2). As with the canoe, the table of offsets is shown two ways, the second being for convenience when building upside down. If you add the measurements between stations you'll see that the boat is really only 15 feet 3⅜ inches long, give or take a little depending on how your plank ends come together. I say "16-foot" because it's easier!

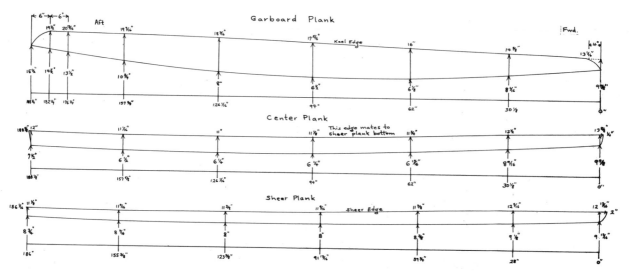

Figure 3-2. Plank drawings for the 16-foot kayak. The exact curves at the plank ends will depend on your particular setup, so cut the planks a little long at first, then fit them as described in Chapter 10.

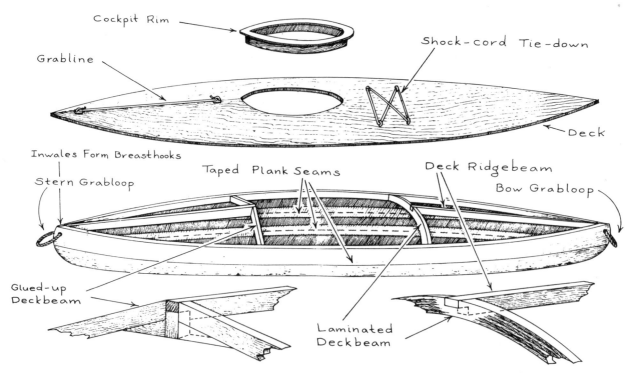

Figure 3-3. Overall view of the 16-foot kayak, showing the option of laminated versus peaked deckbeams.

4. Setting up Shop

Figure 4-1. The ideal workspace. No shop can have enough light. Windows along both long walls are excellent. A wood-floored shop is best. The workspace should be at least 4 feet longer than the boat at either end, and 4 feet or more between the boat and the workbench is also helpful. Shops can be too small, but rarely too big.

Boats have been built in cellars, attics, garages, barns, kitchens, New York City apartments, and on the beach out under the stars. We've all heard stories of windows, doors, and even walls removed on launching day. Boats can be built just about anywhere.

The desire to build a boat can be a powerful thing that sweeps many objections from its path. There are, nonetheless, some minimum requirements. You will need shelter from the elements. Glued and taped construction works only on dry wood, so the old image of the keel and ribs sitting out on the ways covered with snow is out of the picture. In summer an open shed would do, but an enclosed space is better.

If you are using a room in your house, check first by actual measurement to see if you will be able to remove the finished product. If you are building a 14-foot boat, your space has got to be at least a couple of feet longer than this so you can maneuver planks and battens. You'll need side clearance as well, on both sides of the boat, plus room for a bench and yourself. You can lay down some inexpensive plywood or particle board to protect the floor from drips and gouges, and to fasten your forms to if need be.

The important point is that the space be yours for the duration. In the past I have built projects in the kitchen, but it meant a lot of interruption and extra cleaning up.

If I'm called away in the middle of a job, I want to be able just to lay my tools down and walk away. When I come back, the tools and the

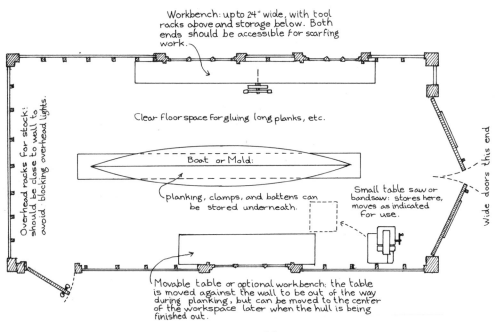

Workbench: up to 24" wide, with tool racks above and storage below. Both ends should be accessible for scarfing work.

Overhead racks for stock: should be close to wall to avoid blocking overhead lights.

Clear floor space for gluing long planks, etc.

Boat or Mold:

planking, clamps, and battens can be stored underneath.

Small table saw or bandsaw: stores here, moves as indicated for use.

Wide doors this end

Movable table or optional workbench: the table is moved against the wall to be out of the way during planking, but can be moved to the center of the workspace later when the hull is being finished out.

work are right where I left them and ready to go. No time is wasted hunting down tools or re-setting plane irons or reclamping a jig. For me this is a great timesaver, and it avoids needless complications and headaches, too.

Having your own space free and clear is also a good way to take the pressure off a completion date.

Time and Money

Time and money are the twin pincers by which Western Civilization crushes us a little each day. They are the two commodities that no one ever has enough of.

Given the wide range of variation among people it is impossible to answer precisely the perennial question, "How long will it take?" I have a friend who can build an 8-foot solo canoe in about 20 hours, while another person might take two or three times as long. Your skill, your need for perfection, and the degree of finish you desire all have to be factored in. The boats in this book will require between 40 and 100 hours, from several weekends to a winter's project.

Two important factors are regularity of effort and the length of uninterrupted time allotted. In one six-hour period, you often can accomplish more than in three two-hour ones, but with foresight you can use several small blocks of time to prepare for a larger one.

The question of how much it will cost is also slippery, because your choice of materials can vary. Since these boats are small, however, the difference in cost between the best materials and adequate materials is insignificant compared with the amount of labor you will have invested. Roughly speaking, these boats should cost between $100 and $200. Setup materials may add a little more, depending on how good a scrounger you are.

The amount you spend on tools will depend on what you need, or think you need. Tools should be thought of as lifetime purchases rather than a per-boat expense.

Your biggest investment is your time, your sweat, and your tears. What you get can be as good or better than any store-bought craft, better tailored to your particular needs and probably better-performing as well.

There are those who feel that the therapeutic value of building something functional and beautiful with their own hands is the best benefit of all. The choice of motivation is yours.

Electrical Power

Once a space has been secured, you are going to need light and power. The power requirements for this type of work are very slight—you do not need large stationary machines, and there is little, if any, milling called for. If you can run an electric drill, you probably have enough power. If you need some heavy cutting, and don't have a bandsaw, a table saw, or radial arm saw, you can always take the work to a local lumberyard or cabinetmaker's shop.

Light

Light is something that you can't get enough of. It has been said that you can work only as well as you can see. This is an obvious but overlooked truth. If you can't see the line you are trying to cut to, then you don't have enough light.

In my own shop I use a series of four-tube fluorescent fixtures overhead for general area illumination, and over my bench I have a row of incandescent bulbs for fill-in. Incandescent is a more restful light, and it's better for close or fine work. I also have at least half a dozen drop lights of the clamp-on type that I use to bring light to any job that is still too dark.

I find that 25-foot extension cords and four-way power outlets are a good way to distribute power around the shop without creating a huge tangle of cords. Overhead power outlets are another way of reducing cord tangle.

While on the subject of light, do not neglect daylight—the best source of all. I try to arrange my benches so they have a lot of window area behind them. Daylight is good light. It's strong, even, and restful for the eyes. It's also about as free as anything gets in this world, and for painting and varnishing it is the only illumination that really gets you the best results.

Heat

If this were the best of all possible worlds, all boatbuilders would live in the tropics, or at least have nicely insulated, affordably heated workshops. Since the realities of the world are harsher than this, and since most boatbuilding projects are undertaken in the winter months, in preparation for good times in the summer ahead, sooner or later you are going to be involved in the search for heat.

Some jobs, like measuring and cutting, may be done in whatever minimum temperature feels adequate for your own comfort. But other processes, such as gluing, require set temperatures for good results. Often the easiest thing to do is to move such jobs into the house, if you can. My family got used to watching TV through a forest of garboards and clamps.

If you can't bring the work to the heat, you have to get clever. A tarp or blanket hung like a tent over a canoe can reduce the area you have to heat to a minimum. A good heat tent won't actually touch the object it

Figure 4-2. Two off-beat methods for delivering safe heat to a glue-up. Below, a metal-shelled drop light is placed over the plank scarf, which is clamped by weight (lead blocks) piled on a pressure pad under the shell. Another lead or wood block holds one side of the shell off the plank to avoid excessive heat buildup. The light bulb (60- to 75-watt) is not touching anything. *The technique can be adapted for gluing other small pieces by substituting a tarp or blanket for the metal shell to enclose the critical area. Above, porcelain or plastic light fixtures on metal or plastic boxes are permanently fastened to a strongback box (described in Chapter 7). Here, the lights are used to heat a canoe on molds with the garboard plank in place. Blankets or tarps are draped over the setup to trap the heat. If necessary, a light wooden framework will hold the tarp away from freshly taped seams. Tarps must not touch bulbs or reflector shells.*

surrounds, but will envelope it in a minimal air space which can be easily heated by light bulbs or possibly an electric space heater.

I've seen heat tents for something as large as a 60-foot trimaran and as small as a 6-square-inch plank scarf. In the latter case, the "tent" is no more than the regular metal reflector shell on a drop light with a 60-watt bulb. The lamp is placed over the scarf with a small air space left open at one end. The bulb is *not* in contact with the wood. With such an arrangement, I have successfully glued scarfs on zero-degree nights in an unheated shop.

Although such a lamp can be safely left on for long periods of time, you should determine for yourself just how long you can leave your specific setup unattended. Check the temperature at regular intervals until you know what to expect.

I do not leave *any* heat setup on while I'm asleep or unable to check on it periodically. You can use timers to turn lights off at midnight and have them back on again by six when you wake up.

Any source of heat other than a properly wired lightbulb makes me nervous. I include infrared heat lamps in this prohibition. Heat lamps can and do start fires if set too close or if they fall or touch something. I've seen a large boatyard swept by a disastrous fire that started from an unattended heat lamp.

Regular lightbulbs take longer to heat a given area, but their heating is more general and pervasive in the long run. They are better suited to making a warm envelope of air that surrounds your work and heats all of it, even those parts not in the direct light. Heat lamps tend to warm just the spot they are shining on, while an area an inch away can be quite cold.

Remember that any heat setup, even a lightbulb under a tarp, is potentially dangerous. Make sure the tarp can't touch the bulbs or even the reflector shields.

For a time I had a big box on pulleys that I could lower over a boat I was working on. It was insulated with 1-inch foam, and used about ten 100-watt bulbs for heat. It was really just an overgrown gradeschool chicken-egg incubator, but it would maintain an 80-degree or better temperature on a mold during a cold New England night. It was a success, but cumbersome.

Then I took the next logical step and used the planked hull itself as the box to hold the heated air. I used blankets to insulate the hull, extending them down to the floor. I ran a string of bulbs right inside the mold, using Romex and porcelain sockets. This worked just as well, and I didn't have any more dreams about a big heavy box hanging over my precious molds and boats like the sword of Damocles.

With this system, it does take some time for the air temperature to build up, and awhile for the wood to heat up from that. So I am generous with my clamping times—around 12 hours of good temperature, maybe more. Of course, the old glue cures more while the next round of planks is clamped up, so by the time the whole planking job is finished the whole boat has been pretty well cooked.

I usually put the leftover glue in its cup in the mold, along with a mocked-up glue piece. I use these, and the squeeze-out, to check on how the glue is setting up. I check the coolest spot in the mold, not the warmest. It's helpful to hang a thermometer or two in the mold to help you locate spots that will take longer to cure.

No matter what your heating setup, it's a good idea to bring assembly pieces into the house ahead of time to warm up, and to keep the glue in the house as a matter of course when the weather turns cold. Cold epoxy is impossible to pour, mix, or work with. A drop light can keep containers of it at a working temperature in a cold shop.

This system is simple and effective. It doesn't cost much to operate and it's reasonably safe. Remember, though, that the burden of intelligent operation is on *you*. The shop you save could be your own.

Tools and Tool Acquisition

The mystique of boatbuilding includes chests full of exotic tools, hopefully inherited from one's grandfather. Fortunately, though, you can get a lot of mileage from just a few basic tools in light plywood construction.

There is a fine line between what is necessary and what is a luxury. Purchase tools only as the need arises, remembering that different methods of work and individual preference mean that two workers doing the same job may use completely different tools.

If you can try out tools in a friend's shop, or through a woodworking course, you have the opportunity to learn before you buy. Talk to other woodworkers, but remember that personal preference and prejudice will abound.

There are several categories of tools, and you will need some from each. The following list is *not* complete, but it is the start of a collection; the boats in this book can be built with them. You may *not* need *all* the tools listed, and you may find that some substitution will be needed for your own particular style of work.

Good tools cost money, but bad tools aren't even a close substitute.

MEASURING AND SETUP
Straightedge (3- or 4-foot)
Metal rulers (6-inch, 12-inch, 36-inch), or a good wooden ruler
Steel tape (20-foot)
Squares (roofing, tee square, draftsman's triangle)
Dividers
Plumb line
Chalkline

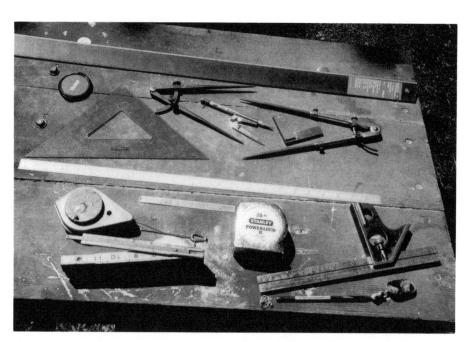

Figure 4-3. Layout tools. A 3-foot steel straightedge is on top. Next are two dividers and a pencil compass or "scriber." Measuring tools include 30-inch and 6-inch rules, a wood folding ruler, and a 25-foot steel tape, as well as a combination square and a chalkline. A lens cap and an inspection mirror snuck into the picture.

SAWS
Fret saw or bucksaw
Small circular saw, bandsaw, jigsaw, or saber saw
Coping saw
Table saw (optional)

Figure 4-4. Saws. An inexpensive Sears jigsaw with scrolling is at the left. Two sizes of backsaws—with homemade Masonite blade guards—are included, as is a 4½-inch worm-drive circular saw. The last tool was used in place of a bandsaw to cut all the planking for the boats in this book, as well as about 90 percent of all the other cutting chores. An expensive tool, but a worker.

PLANES
Small block plane with adjustable throat
Small rabbet plane (No. 90, Stanley)
Medium rabbet plane (No. 93, Stanley)
Scrub plane (preferably in metal) with radiused profile cutter
Smooth No. 3, No. 4 planes
Jointer plane (optional)
3¼-inch electric hand plane (optional)

Figure 4-5. A selection of planes. Starting in the foreground and going clockwise: a 22-inch jointer, a 9-inch smooth, a scrub, a 3¼-inch electric plane, a block plane, a No. 93 rabbet, and a No. 90 rabbet. The scrub plane was used extensively in scarfing, fairing, and planing planks to the line. The smooth plane and the two rabbets were also helpful, and the jointer was used to finish all the scarfs right after the scrub.

CHISELS
¼-inch, ½-inch, 1-inch wood chisels Fishtail gouge (available from any woodcraft supply house, many of which ship by mail. See the Appendix.)

Figure 4-6. Chisels and gouges. Left to right: a fishtail gouge (a small-craft builder's adze) and a bent gouge of the "London" pattern, both of which have the bevel on the outside, making them very controllable; a 1-inch paring chisel; a 2-inch mortising chisel; and a ¼-inch mortising chisel. In the foreground, a wooden mallet for driving them when needed.

DRILL
⅜-inch variable-speed electric drill and drill bits Countersink Bore Screwdriver bits

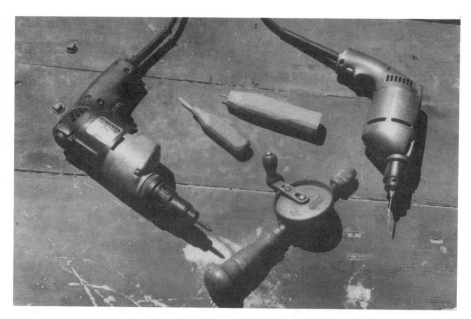

Figure 4-7. Drills and drilling: An electric drill and a small egg-beater type are shown. The wood-handled objects are homemade awls, good for small screws in light wood. One uses an old three-cornered sail needle, while the other is just a brad in a handle. To use, spin while pressing down. An electric screwgun is included too.

RASPS
Nicholson Cabinet-maker pattern, No. 49 and No. 50

MISCELLANEOUS
Hammer Screwdrivers Utility knife Sharpening stones

Figure 4-8. Miscellaneous. The ever-helpful belt sander is on the top, along with a steel rafter square. A rubber hand-sanding block is on the right, along with a cabinetmaker's pattern rasp and a four-in-hand that has rough and smooth teeth, flat and round all in the same tool.

On the other side is an inspection mirror (good for checking joints in tight quarters), as well as a depth gauge and a small bevel gauge, both homemade, and a plumb-bob. There are two lead pigs, good for holding battens or applying clamping pressure. There is a plywood scrap pressure pad under the lower of the two.

Having the right tools will make the job easier, but one tool may often be substituted for another in a pinch.

Battens

There are some special tools that the boatbuilder needs to do his particular job. Battens—long strips of variously dimensioned wood—fit into this category.

As we shall see, curves and boats go together. To lay out the curves and to draw them you use battens, either to help you eyeball a curve, or to guide your pencil.

Battens are best made from even-grained pieces of softwood like spruce, fir, or pine. They should be smooth and evenly dimensioned. Get them ripped out on a good table saw—this is no place for wavy edges.

Battens vary in size and shape depending on the job they have to perform. Some may be flat and wide, say ¾ inch by ⁵⁄₃₂ inch, while others may be quite square. The wide, flat one has less tendency to move sideways from its fair curve, but it may not take every curve. The square one will take bends more easily but isn't always right either.

If there is a lot of twist in a plank, that is, if it changes from horizontal at the 'midships point to nearly vertical at the ends, the wide batten will more accurately reflect the way the plank will lay in this spot because it will be more affected by the twist than a narrow batten will be.

You may be able to get long rippings as scrap from a cabinetshop or lumberyard, if you check around. Otherwise buy a length of good straight-grained pine and saw it up as needed.

Good battens are worth protecting. Don't nail through them if you can help it. Hold them in place with weight, or a nail driven alongside; especially in light stock, a nail passing through it can distort the grain.

Store battens on the floor out of the way, or on a rack. Don't let them get excessively bent or kinked. You can work with or against a gentle bend, but kinked battens are useless.

Clamps

Boatbuilders never have enough clamps. Even though the method of building given here reduces your need for clamps, there are times—as when you are putting on a rail—when there is no substitute for a lot of clamps.

Eventually, buying a clamp or two at a time, you will build up a collection. In my shop, variety is the key. Clamps range from 12-inch sliding bars and 6-inch C's down to little C's, wooden cam clamps, and dozens of spring clamps.

Each type has its own advantages and disadvantages. Some are good for one-handed application, while others don't vibrate loose as easily. Some are too large and heavy, or just the wrong shape for certain applications. All this can only come clear with experience.

Figure 4-9. Clamps. The biggest C-clamp has about 18 inches of depth and a 24-inch throat. The smallest is 1½ inches. A spring clamp and several sizes and types of bar clamps are also shown.

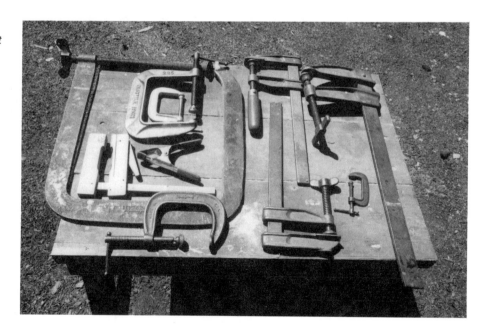

If you work alone you'll have to learn to clamp with one hand, using your knees, hips, elbows, or forehead to get that extra bit of pressure. You'll learn to jump lively when they start dropping to the floor, as they sometimes do.

You'll learn to start clamping long boards from the middle, or to use a clamped-on leg for extra support out on the end. You'll learn to use a pencil gauge mark to get things in the right place so you won't end up 3 inches shy of the stem when the last clamp goes on.

You'll learn to use weight, shores, or screws and nails—even string and wedges—to do the job a clamp can't or won't do. Some of today's boatbuilding tricks are the same ones used in the Neolithic forests of Europe or on the banks of the Nile thousands of years ago.

You can—and will—learn to make your own clamping jigs and fixtures. It's all part of the game.

The only problem is . . . you'll never have enough clamps—ever.

Workbenches

Among cabinetmakers the workbench is an article of faith. It is an elaborate affair with lots of vises and dogs, built like a rock.

For light plywood work, I have found that my needs are really quite different. I actually require two distinct types of bench.

One of them is a scarfing and plank bench about 36 inches high. It should be freestanding, or at least have its ends away from any walls, but should be sturdy enough not to rock as you work on it. The bench does not have to be overly long because the curves of most planks make a long, straight bench not so useful. Instead, I use one that is about 8 feet long and place small, movable T-shaped floor fixtures to support the overhanging ends of the planks. I move the plank forward and back on the bench to get support for the area that I'm currently working on, clamping it into position.

Because of the curved nature of the planks, the bench can be quite narrow, just enough to allow for a 12-inch-wide board. A bench any wider is a waste of space.

I need a good flat surface to work on and to support a scarf while I'm cutting it. I use a particle board top on my bench for this, but a suitable scrap of plywood under the end would work too, as long as you block the rest of the plank up along the bench in a similar manner. The edge of this surface should be sharp and square so that the thin edge of the scarf is well supported while it is being cut.

I use a clamp or two to hold the plank in place while I'm working it. I find that 36 inches off the floor is a good height for me when I'm hand-planing, but you should choose the height that is best suited for you. The bench should be steady enough so that it *will not rock* while you are working.

It is not really necessary to build a special bench for planking. If you already have a sturdy, well-braced set of sawhorses, you can put a 2 × 10 or 2 × 12 over them and it will serve quite well in most cases. You may need to clamp the board to one or both horses to stop its creeping while scarfing, especially if your plane is set too deep.

The scarfing and planking bench needs to be accessible from all sides to be really efficient. This is because pairs of planks are mirror images, and you will need to cut different scarfs on different faces of the plank. Add in the fact that you probably handle tools better on one side than another, and you will appreciate all the angles you can get.

The other bench I find useful is really an assembly table. I have an old exterior door covered with particle board and waxed to resist glue. It measures about 3 feet by 7 feet. This gives me a good flat surface on which to place hulls that need to be trimmed out, sanded, or painted. A bit of carpet makes excellent padding. The bench also serves as a perfect surface on which to glue up a number of scarfed planks at once.

So far there has been no mention of vises. I do have one long, wall-mounted workbench, about 18 inches wide and 20 feet long. This has a bench vise in the center of its length, and it is very useful for making breasthooks, but this is almost the only operation that calls for using a vise on a regular basis.

Racks

It seems that I am forever making racks in my shop, mostly of the overhead variety. They hold battens, plank patterns, plank and rail stock, and just about everything else. They help keep clutter off the floor and give a badly needed measure of organization to an area that otherwise exhibits a primordial chaos.

I have racks and shelves for my tools as well, but they really don't spend much time on them. The tools I use live on the job. They're on molds, on benches, and in the hulls. I like to keep them right where they get used. If all the tools are back on their shelves it means either a major cleanup, or that I'm trying to impress someone.

This system works for me, but you may want or need a more organized approach. It is important that you work out your own particular style, and this will naturally occur. The point is simply that there aren't any rules—just do what you have to in order to get the job done.

5. Drawing

I t has been said that if you can draw a boat you can build it. Lofting is the name given to the process in which all parts of the vessel—their shapes, angles, and bevels—are drawn out full size before any building is done. The interaction and interconnection between each piece is rigorously examined, so that, in effect, you have built the boat in your mind before you cut your first piece of wood.

Although lofting skills are needed for adapting many existing canoe and kayak designs for building with the taped-seam method (see the Appendix), you will not need to go to quite such lengths to build the boats in this book. Their lofting has already been done and scaled drawings of each piece are provided. You will still need some drawing skills, however, if only to understand the drawings and to reproduce the mold and plank shapes full size (as discussed in Chapters 7 and 10, respectively) preparatory to cutting actual pieces.

Offsets

Lofting usually involves working with offsets. An offset is merely a way of describing the location of a point in reference to a fixed, known point. Most drawings use horizontal baselines and vertical station lines in a Cartesian coordinate system. These are the X and Y axes on a normal graph, or the latitude and longitude lines on a map.

Usually vertical distances are given as heights in inches above the baseline, while the forwardmost or aftermost perpendicular station line is a standard reference for horizontal distance. For example, a point might be located 2 feet aft of the forwardmost perpendicular and 6 inches above the baseline. It is now precisely defined as to location.

Offsets are listed in shorthand form in a table of offsets. By convention, 2.7.1. means 2 feet, 7 inches, and ⅛ of an inch. Similarly, 0.6.4. would be no feet, 6 inches, and ⁴⁄₈ (better known as a half-inch).

The Grid

It follows that a drawing of a boat is usually superimposed on a grid made up of horizontal and vertical reference lines. The grid may be large enough to include the entire boat, or small enough for just one specific part. A long horizontal baseline intersected by regularly spaced verticals may serve as a grid on which to draw out the curve of a given plank.

It's important to select a good drawing surface. Paper is fragile and doesn't take well to multiple erasures. In larger pieces, paper is unwieldy and subject to size variation through changes in atmospheric moisture.

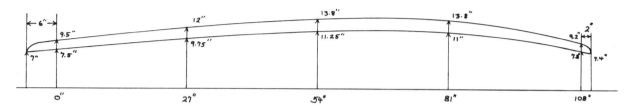

Figure 5-1. A grid consisting of a baseline and five perpendicular "stations" upon which a plank curve is drawn. All measurements are to the bottom edge of the plank. For the sake of clarity, top measurements are omitted. Horizontal distances are given from station 0. Station spacing is 27 inches in this case. Any curved line can be described and drawn with this technique.

Traditional lofting takes place on a painted wood floor, and plywood panels serve the purpose quite well today. (To save time and material, plank shapes for the boats in this book should be drawn directly on the stock from which they will be cut, and the same applies to the molds.)

Mylar in sheets or in rolls is excellent too, but it is not as cheap or as easily available.

Straight Lines

It goes without saying that to be accurate, a grid must be made up of straight lines. Many people claim they can't draw a straight line, and in fact, drawing a long, straight line is not easy. The best way is to use a chalkline tightly stretched between two points. Lift vertically and snap, and the resulting line will be as straight as you can wish for.

A chalkline is pretty thick, so you will have to pick one side or the other of the line for your reference; otherwise you will have the thickness of the line as a plus or minus error in the drawing.

I like to use a chalkline that is very lightly chalked, and I even snap off the excess in the air before using it. This gives a finer line to start with. Since chalk rubs off easily, it's a good idea to use a metal straightedge to make a pencil line along one edge of the chalkline as a permanent reference. Use a metal straightedge for shorter lines as well—wooden yardsticks or rulers may be bowed imperceptibly.

Perpendiculars and Parallel Lines

If you liked plane geometry, you will love setting up the grid. After getting the baseline, the next step is erecting the first perpendicular.

You can use a large square, but I prefer to use the classic Euclidian method with some long dividers, because I feel it is a more accurate way to proceed.

Since error has a way of creeping in I usually erect only one perpendicular in this way. If I need others, I draw them parallel to the original

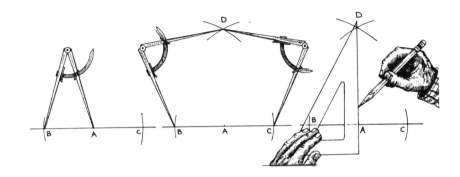

Figure 5-2. Drawing perpendicular lines. (1) Use the point at which you wish to erect the perpendicular as the center of an arc, which you swing through the baseline on either side, drawing short, intersecting segments at B and C. (2) With the dividers set wider than the length AB, swing arcs using B and C as centerpoints, with the arcs intersecting at D. (3) Line DA is perpendicular to baseline BC.

perpendicular, but only after drawing lines parallel to the baseline. This avoids the embarrassment of having the various perpendiculars all leaning at slightly different angles to one another.

In setting up lines parallel to the baseline, the first step I take is to measure up my first perpendicular and mark a point. Then I mark another point for the other end of the new line the same distance off the baseline. This point needs to be located with the measuring device square to the baseline, so that the two lines will be truly parallel. I snap a line between these two points and check by measurement at several points to see that it is indeed parallel to the base. If it isn't I try again. When all is well, I pencil this line in. Now I can draw in lines parallel to the first perpendicular by measuring from it the same distance along the upper and lower baselines, and connecting those points with a straightedge.

I check each line by measurement as it is drawn, and don't proceed until everything checks out accurately.

This may seem like the long way around the barn, but it works and seems to have the least cumulative error for me.

Measurement

We have already seen that accurate measurement is critical. How can we achieve such a standard?

First, don't trust your steel tape with its sloppy end hook, and be even more suspicious if you are using more than one steel tape. They can vary by as much as $\frac{1}{16}$ inch quite easily, due to play in the hook. Use a good-quality steel ruler or use the 1-inch mark on the tape rather than the end hook. Remember to subtract the extra inch if you do this!

Sometimes you can nail a strip of wood or a stop block of some kind to the lofting platform so that you can automatically butt your ruler or tick strip (see below) to the same point on your reference line each time. In addition to ensuring accuracy, it can be a real timesaver if you work alone.

One way to attain accuracy is not to measure at all! Forget the numbers, and just deal in intervals. If the space is small you can use dividers to recreate that spacing somewhere else. You don't need to know how many inches it is, but you can accurately reproduce it nonetheless.

For intervals too large for your dividers, you can use flat wooden strips called tick strips. These have one end squared off so they will neatly and accurately butt to a stop block or line in a consistent manner.

After the strip is in place, mark the position of the point with a pencil, being sure to label its point of origin and note whether it is a horizontal or a vertical line. Transfer the measurement by butting the strip to your reference line and marking the drawing at the correct pencil mark on the strip.

This is a good way to store and use a lot of measurements all at once. You can take all the sheer heights from the base at once, for example, and then transfer them in a batch, which can save time and confusion. Just be sure to label the tick strips and the points so that you know exactly what each point actually is.

Curved Lines

After the grid is finished, you won't be drawing too many more straight lines. So you'll need some battens and you will have to begin educating your eye.

Once you have plotted the points that make up a curve—the sheer, for example—you sweep your batten through them. Anchor the batten

Figure 5-3. Using a batten to draw curved lines.

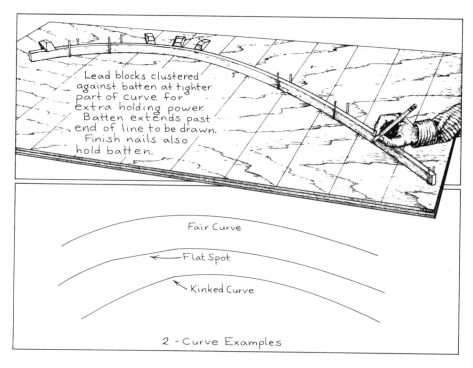

with weights or with small brads alongside it. Try not to nail through it, since that will ruin the wood. The batten may not be able to connect each point and still be in a fair curve. Sight it from each end; if it looks kinked or has some hard spots, loosen up the batten at that point and let it spring to where it wants. Sometimes changing an end will affect the curve farther down.

If one or several points are slightly off the mark, the cause might be either a drawing error or a slight irregularity in the grid. Small, isolated differences can be "absorbed" into the building process, but large or consistent errors should be checked carefully.

When the curve looks right, use the batten to guide your pencil and draw in the line. When this is done, take the batten off and sight the actual line. If it still looks good, then alright. If it isn't, erase, rebatten, and redraw until it is correct.

Not all battens are suited for all curves. You may need a thin, thick, wide, or narrow one to get the curve you need. You may need to use several battens to draw one curve if the radius of the curve changes enough, and you will also need to hold the batten at more closely spaced intervals as the curve tightens.

Don't settle for the first curve your batten gives you; get the curve you want, or at least the closest you can get. Change battens if need be. Remember, though, that the batten doesn't lie, and that you have to go with a fair curve.

Patterns

As mentioned, no lofting is required by this book, and since the measurements I provide for the 11-foot canoe and the 16-foot kayak have already been lofted and faired, you can draw the mold and plank shapes full-size directly on the building stock, without bothering to make patterns first. In fact, if you elect to use taped stems and keels, thus eliminating the optional wooden structures, you may not need to make any patterns at all in building the boats in this book, with one exception: I do recommend that you use the false stem patterns as described in Chapter 7. You may also want to make a pattern for a cockpit rim, or a paddle blade that you want to repeat, so a brief discussion of patternmaking is in order.

I find that thin plywood such as ¼-inch Lauan makes excellent pattern stock. Thin paneling is excellent too and is sometimes on sale for a few dollars a sheet. I don't recommend Masonite because it is hard to keep a clean edge while working it. For the false stem patterns I use thicker stock; ⅝- or ¾-inch plywood is excellent, and you are likely to have some left over from making the building platform (Chapter 7) or the molds themselves.

Almost any of the shapes you need to draw are based on some type of grid with a baseline and perpendiculars. Just draw that grid onto the pattern stock and lay out the shape from there.

Stem patterns are usually drawn inside an area defined by the baseline and the forwardmost (or aftermost) perpendicular. The points of the curve are defined as their perpendicular distances from these two references. For the 11-foot canoe, measurements are made upward at 3-inch intervals along the baseline, and outward (parallel to the baseline) at 3-inch intervals along the perpendicular. A fair curve through the resulting points defines the stem outline. (See Figure 2-4.)

In cutting out a pattern it is important not to cut inside your line. Cut closely to the line and plane down right to it. Check curved lines for fairness, and straight lines for bumps or hollows.

It is hard to have too much information on a pattern. In addition to labeling it as to what the shape is and what boat it belongs to, you will do well to include any and all reference lines that can be used to orient the workpiece on the pattern, or to align the workpiece to the boat or mold. Transfer these lines to the workpiece or they won't do you any good.

6. Materials and Scantlings

E very builder, consciously or not, develops a philosophy of materials whereby all the variables of availability, cost, difficulty in working or handling, and aesthetics are given their proper weighting.

Small boats are labor-intensive. This means that materials are only a fraction of your overall investment. It would be a mistake to invest a lot of time on a project that is built from materials of questionable quality. Use the best materials you can afford.

It makes sense to use local sources of supply, since most of the materials called for in this book are readily available. This will save you time and money. If certain specialty items cannot be found in your area, you can have them shipped to you. (See the Appendix for a list of suppliers I have dealt with successfully by mail.)

Wood

Wood is one of man's oldest construction materials, and still one of the most versatile and useful. Wood's major drawback in boatbuilding lies in its susceptibility to rot.

Proper construction, modern coatings, and care can largely overcome this. Fortunately for our purposes, the rot problem is more pronounced in larger, decked structures that use bigger pieces. In general, small, light craft like canoes and kayaks are on the water only when in use and are stored in a dry place, reducing this problem to insignificance.

There are enormous advantages to wood. It offers the highest strength-to-weight ratios this side of carbon fibers. Wood is resilient and flexible, and failures due to fatigue (repeated flexing) are nonexistent.

Wood is at once stiff and strong—due to its cell and grain structure—and is easily worked and bent.

It fastens easily via mechanical fasteners or glue, and requires no special conditions in the workplace. It is cost-effective and widely available. All told, it is an altogether suitable material for the one-off builder with average shop facilities.

We will be working with both natural woods and plywoods. In this style of building, plywood is used as planking and decking material, while natural wood is reserved for structural members and trim.

Natural Wood

For structural members—keel, stems, rails, coamings, etc.—natural wood is unsurpassed for strength coupled with light weight.

Of the many woods suitable for boatbuilding, softwoods are most attractive in terms of their light weight. Of these spruce leads the pack, followed by Douglas fir and white cedar.

Spruce is incredibly light and strong. To get good, clear lengths you will probably need to buy Sitka spruce from a specialty boat-lumber yard. It will be expensive but worth it. I would not hesitate to use this wood exclusively for the keel, stems, and rails.

Common lumberyard spruce hides out under the name of furring strips or strapping and staging planks. It will probably be knotty and wet, but the occasional clear or nearly clear piece (small pin knots are not bad in moderation) will be a bargain, perfectly acceptable for use when you can't find Sitka.

No Latin names are needed here—all spruces are strong and glue well when dry. Spruce is not tremendously rot resistant, so it will require protection such as paint or varnish.

Clear, vertical-grained fir is one of the joys of woodworking, and it is good for boats, though heavier than spruce or cedar. It glues and works well, though it has a slight tendency to splinter. It can be found as stair-tread material in lengths up to 20 feet. Fir can be substituted for spruce anywhere, although I'd increase the deckbeam scantlings slightly if I were using fir there. Avoid slash-grained fir, in which the grain runs side to side across the piece rather than up and down through its thickness.

White and Atlantic cedars are light and strong, and bend better than spruce or fir. They are good for light parts where no great inherent strength is needed. A laminated cockpit rim would be a suitable use, but a deckbeam would not be.

Other woods to consider, especially for rails and breasthooks, might include the mahoganies or a hardwood such as cherry, maple, or ash. Oak is good too, especially in smaller pieces. The extra durability and attractive grain of hardwood is nice for rails, and the extra weight is not critical. I find cherry to be one of the nicest woods for this application. Don't be a typical boatbuilder and use oak just because you think you ought to.

Most of wood's strength and weakness comes from the grain. Strength is best with the grain and least across it. Especially in boatwork, where curves predominate, you should be careful to see that you don't lay out pieces with weak cross-grain portions. Time and time again we will see that wood fails where stress has been applied across the grain.

When bending wood, it is good to remember that it bends easiest along the run of the grain rather than across it. As a practical matter, though, the materials you are working with here are small enough that they should dry-bend into any necessary shape. Steam or other special techniques are not needed.

Lumber should be neatly stacked or piled. Unless it is really dry, it should be stacked with spacers evenly distributed to promote good air flow. Keep it out of the rain and sun and away from areas of poor ventilation and high humidity.

Plywood

Plywood consists of stacked veneers of alternating grain direction glued up into panels. Sometimes the veneers are also separated by one of a variety of core materials. This could be either a thicker veneer or a sheet of end-grain material. Since plywood is manufactured, you can pretty much predict the quality of a given product from a given manufacturer. Grown timber, by contrast, requires careful hand picking to ensure a given level of acceptable quality.

The most important qualities that we will need from our plywood are:

■ no voids in the inner plies
■ resistance to delamination
■ suitability of veneers to marine environment

Plywoods are manufactured to a wealth of specifications and grades, and they are not all created equal. It's a good idea to read the trade literature and speak to a reputable dealer before making any purchases. The number and thickness of veneers that make up a panel are usually (but not invariably) an indication of quality. A panel made up of five veneers (two on each side of a center sheet) is usually stronger than one the same thickness made of only three veneers. It will also weigh more and have different bending characteristics.

Some plywoods are made specifically for marine use. These panels are usually classified AB, meaning that they have an excellent veneer on one face and a slightly imperfect one on the other. They are made (or in some cases claimed to be made) without voids, and of course, cost more. Exterior-grade plywood uses the same glues as the marine grade but is apt to have too many voids for our purposes.

The European marine plywoods are premium. Their choice of glues and veneers is excellent and they come in a variety of thicknesses from 3 to 4 millimeters up to one inch or better. These panels have excellent finishing qualities and are generally quite durable. They are far and away the best choice for plywood planking stock, and not overly expensive in the quantities these boats need.

Domestic fir marine plywood is not as good a choice. The thinnest panel available is ¼ inch, which is rather on the thick, heavy side for lightweight construction. It also has finishing problems, mainly because of raised grain.

One-quarter-inch Lauan plywood is readily available at most lumberyards and is another possible choice where low cost is essential and quality is not a primary consideration. While as thick as fir ply, it is lighter in weight. Lauan has a thick core of end-grain material, but is somewhat stronger than you might at first suspect. Since it is prone to delamination and darkening from water, it is probably best glassed over as a matter of course. I have a friend who has built quite a few canoes and kayaks from this material—all sheathed—and they have proven inexpensive and serviceable.

Handling. Plywood should be stored absolutely flat to minimize sheet curling. I usually cut the standard 4- by 8-foot sheets down to 2 by 8 feet as soon as I get back from the lumberyard, to simplify storing and handling. (An alternative is to have the yard cut the sheet for you for a nominal charge.)

Many lumberyards will deliver for free. Here's what I've done when I've had to transport plywood myself without a pickup truck. I used a simple roof rack, just the bars-across-the-roof, clamp-to-the-rain-gutter type. Four-millimeter plywood or even ¼-inch is pretty flexible, so unless I was buying enough to make a thick stack (10 sheets or so), I would bring a couple of 2 × 4s to go lengthwise under the plywood on the rack and support it.

Clamping the leading edge of the plywood stack between some 1 × 3 furring strips solidifies it and makes it less liable to be bent up and back by the wind; at highway speeds, thin plywood can do some outrageous things. Use C-clamps; they are much less liable to vibrate off. As a bonus, the C-clamps will make good tie-down points. If you can bend the plywood down slightly, wind pressure will help hold it *on* the rack rather than trying to lift it off.

I found that tie-downs to the front and rear bumpers were just as important as tie-downs across the rack. Finding a chafe-free attachment to the bumper is important. Drilling a hole and using an eyebolt is one solution. Using a heavier rope or nylon web strap looped over it is another. Lumberyard twine, while free, is very prone to chafe, so a little protection goes a long way.

Cutting. The main problem in cutting plywood comes from splinters ripping out from the top or bottom veneer, depending on the type of saw you use. This is at its worst when cutting across the grain. If only one side of the work is to show, you can get by with marking and taking your cut on the appropriate side.

For a neater job, score your marked line with a *sharp* utility knife before you cut. For precision in finicky work, score both top and bottom. Now cut just to the "outside" or waste side of the line. This will confine the splintering to the area outside your workpiece.

It's always good to preserve the line as you cut; otherwise, the cut may wander back and forth by the thickness of the saw blade. It's better to be outside the line and to have to plane the wood down a little than to come inside the line and lose some of the workpiece. Saw cuts are a little rough anyway and usually need dressing down with a sharp plane to be of finish quality.

I use a circular saw for cutting large sheets, setting it only a little deeper than the plywood is thick. I place 2 × 4 scraps lying flat to keep the plywood from sagging and binding the cut. You could use a blade made for plywood, but I find that carbide teeth hold up longer.

If you use a saber saw, make sure the panel is well supported and held down against the cut. These saws are especially prone to tearing out grain, so you may want to make the cuts a little more oversized to compensate.

If you have access to a big bandsaw the cuts are easily made, but you will need a big enough throat size to make 24-inch cuts.

The 2- by 8-foot sheets of plywood can go into overhead racks or slip under a bench. One good place to store them—or any other long rippings—might be right under the mold that you are working on. It's surprising how this spot can be so convenient and yet not underfoot. If you do store materials under the mold, be careful of glue drips. Covering the stock with a layer or two of old newspaper will protect it quite well.

Scantlings for plywood. Due to its cross-grained structure, a given thickness of plywood will be stronger than the same thickness of natural wood. Whereas ½ or ⅜ inch is a normal thickness for cedar planks in small craft, the equivalent plywood planking would be either ¼ inch in fir or Lauan, or 4 millimeters in a quality imported panel. Since plywood is heavier than an equivalent piece of natural wood, it's important to keep these sizes in mind or your boat will be a real barge.

Planking with plywood. Some people like plywood and some people hate it. Aside from blind prejudice, the latter's dislike probably stems from two main sources.

Plywood edges are one-half end-grain and will absorb water quickly. This can lead to delamination, leading to rot and a loss of structural integrity. Unless the edges are capped and sealed, some delamination is probably inevitable, especially if the wood is subject to the increased stress of cycling through wet and dry, hot and cold that comes from being stored outside. This single factor has probably turned more people off to plywood than anything else. This is a valid objection, but it's worth noting that the quality imported plywoods are much, much less susceptible to this type of failure—almost to the point of negligibility.

Another drawback is that normal marine fir plywood does not finish very well. It tends to check in the sun and show raised grain, largely due to the slash-grain fir used in the top veneers. Using a sealer before painting will help, but it is wiser to use a better-quality plywood to begin with.

Fiberglass

Fiberglass offers the builder some excellent properties. It is available in several configurations, including chopped-strand mat, woven roving, unwoven roving, and cloth, but I use cloth exclusively on these boats. The cloth itself comes in a variety of weights, which range from about 1 to 10 ounces per square yard. It comes in rolls up to 38 inches wide and in narrow tapes, which are particularly useful for reinforcing and sealing seams. I order cloth by mail from Defender Industries (address in Appendix), but it is available from local wholesalers and retailers around the country as well as from other mail-order suppliers.

A major use for cloth is as a sheathing material to protect against abrasion or to seal and waterproof. Fiberglass over plywood is one of the best ways to make light, strong decks.

Another major advantage of the plywood/glass combination is the increased strength that results. The 23 percent increase in weight that sheathing adds—and this figure can be less—can increase resistance to failure by one-third or more, and increase the amount of deflection before failure up to nearly 50 percent.

Although I may sheathe a kayak's deck, I prefer not to sheathe tack-and-tape hulls, except for the garboard planks (see below). Some people prefer to sheathe the entire boat, and if you are using Lauan plywood this may be the best way to protect a wood that isn't otherwise suitable for the marine environment.

I have used the term "fiberglass" rather loosely as a synonym for all reinforcing fabrics. Besides the standard, inexpensive fiberglass configurations already mentioned, there are Dynel, Xynol, Vectra, and Kevlar cloths, the latter being composed of aramid fibers rather than spun glass. Some types are more elastic and adapt to curves and compound shapes better than others. Differing cloths have different wet-out needs and different strength characteristics. No single kind has all the advantages, since superiority in one category—say abrasion resistance—may mean that it is difficult to sand and smooth. Some cloths may be relatively fragile when applied to a flexible substrate, while some may be difficult to control given the amount of resin they absorb.

I use a single layer of very light (1.2-ounce) fiberglass cloth to sheathe the keel and garboard planks, and I reinforce this with tape on the keel to protect against abrasion. The cloth is little more than a matrix for the epoxy resin to adhere to. The tape can be applied in as many layers as desired. It's a simple system, and works well, but I do not claim it is the only one.

There is a great deal of literature on the subject of cloths and sheathing. Some useful sources are listed in the Appendix. Reading manufacturers' literature and speaking with other builders will show you the various options and give you an idea of cost, availability, and ease of application.

Glues and fillers are covered in Chapter 8. Suffice it to say here that I use epoxy resin for sheathing and taping, and a thickened epoxy glue for filling seams. Polyester resins and glues simply do not bond tenaciously enough with wood, and besides, you need the superior gap-filling qualities of epoxy in the seams. Taping epoxy-filled seams with cloth wetted out with polyester resin is a doubly bad idea because polyester does not bond well with cured epoxy. In short, epoxy is three times as expensive as polyester, but it's worth it, and a $30 gallon is more than enough for a boat.

Scantlings

By "scantlings" we mean the dimensions of the structural members of a boat or ship—the thickness of the planking, the width and depth of the keel or ribs, and so forth. There are mathematical rules that allow one to calculate the needed sizes and to maintain the correct proportion between elements, but many of these are irrelevant to the small-craft builder.

For small craft in general, and specifically for canoes and kayaks, the essentials are common sense, a good eye for proportion, and the ability to extrapolate from existing models.

A boat is a collection of interacting parts. If any one is out of proportion with the others, trouble can result. In traditional construction, stress is collected and absorbed by the fasteners, the planking, the frames, and the keel, to mention a few components. If any of these fails to do its job, the cumulative stress gets passed on to some other part or parts, which may or may not be adequate to take it on. In lightly built structures, the failure of one part can rapidly snowball into a series of failures.

Unless weight is hypercritical—and it rarely is except in military or racing craft—it is good to build in a certain safety factor.

The balance of weight versus strength was achieved by the old boatbuilders by first making their boats strong, and then gradually paring down the scantlings, guided by a use/failure ratio. This kind of evolution is not achieved overnight, but it does result in boats that are well made and right for their particular circumstances.

This is one of the reasons it is good to review examples from the past to see what they have to show us. For our purposes, the light canoes from the late 1890s provide a wealth of information.

In glued construction, however, the pieces of a boat are more solidly fastened than if they were mechanically joined. A glued plywood boat is essentially one piece of wood, because the glue joints are stronger than the wood itself. This means that some of the old concepts are not valid, and it is possible to build a boat that does not have a keel, stems, or frames. All a glued boat needs are planks and some kind of rail.

Scantlings for the planking are a good place to start, since planking accounts for about 90 percent of such a boat's structure. Four millimeters is the best thickness of plywood to use for canoes and kayaks.

Planking this light is pretty flexible. Bending in a rail of normal dimensions—say ¾ by ½ inch—is overkill and may distort your hull. Likewise, a short, heavy block for a backrest may create a "hard" spot nowhere near as flexible as the rest of the structure. This spot becomes a stress concentrator and a potential trouble area.

Rails glued to the full length of the sheer plank gain a lot of strength from this, especially in the vertical plane, so they don't need to be really heavy. In a small, open canoe, somewhere around 9/16 inch square is fine, and you could go down to less, say 3/8 inch in depth by 1/2 inch in width (the width being greater than the depth to better resist bending in a horizontal plane). An improvement on this is a girder-rail consisting of two 3/8- by 1/2-inch rails, an inwale and a gunwale, separated by small blocks. A girder-rail (see Figure 11-14) is much more able to resist horizontal deflection, and in fact, would be the major structural element in the boat.

Decked boats like a kayak can afford to have an inwale only about 1/2 or 5/8 inch deep and about 5/16 inch thick, possibly less if it doesn't have to hold screws. Remember that the thickness of the planking is functionally a part of this piece.

Plywood is quite stiff in an edgewise direction, so the boat doesn't need the kind of antihogging (sagging) strength that traditional keels and sheer structures were called on to supply. Instead, the real need is to resist deflection on the flat. The function of the keel is reduced to a gluing surface for joining the lower edges of the garboards. Fiberglass tape can serve this same function quite well, and the keel can easily be left out. If you go this route, use three layers of tape and fair them into the planks—particularly at the ends—with epoxy fillets. If used, a typical light canoe keel would be 5/8 inch to 1/2 inch thick and about 1 1/4 inches wide amidships, tapered at the ends. It could be narrower if you like, but this width gives a better landing to step on when entering and leaving the boat.

A laminated stem might be only 1/2 inch wide and about 3/4 inch deep or less, depending on the bevel needed to fit the plank. This will be quite strong, especially in conjunction with the planking.

In traditional building, structural members were sized to accept fasteners. They had to have a minimum width and depth to hold a screw or rivet. In glued construction, your major concern is bonding area in the glue joint.

For breasthooks, which tie the plank ends and stem of a boat together, a thin, 1/4-inch block would probably work. But that 1/4-inch thickness makes for a very thin, fragile glue joint. By using a thicker piece you get a more extensive glued area and, as a bonus, the thicker piece looks better as well.

Because of the flexibility of the planking, you will want enough length to make the glue joint between the planking and the breasthook effective, and this means at least 4 inches. All things being equal, a longer glue joint is probably longer-lived because it holds down "working" of the joint better than a short joint, even if their glued areas are about the same. The place where the inwale and breasthook join is important too, because there is a change in the flexibility of the structure at this point. One or two inches of overlap will strengthen this joint.

Relative size and thickness is worth watching. As a gross example, it makes no sense for a 1-inch-deep rail to join a ¼-inch-thick breasthook, nor would it make sense to mate 4-millimeter planking to a massive keel.

Strength and weight are not always the same. The light girder rail mentioned earlier will do a better job than a heavier, solid piece. Keep in mind the type and direction of the forces that are in play. In a beam that seeks to resist vertical bending, increasing depth is helpful, while making it thicker plays almost no part in this ability. Why pay a penalty for weight when there is no gain in strength?

For instance, a laminated deckbeam in a kayak will get its strength from depth and only needs enough width for efficient gluing to the deck and inwale.

If you examine the deckbeam in the light of function, you will see that its purpose is to resist downward deflection. This deflection can only take place if the sides of the boat spread apart at this place. The deck itself acts as a web membrane, which also helps limit this tendency to spread. Thus, the two parts—deck and deckbeam—are performing mutually beneficial tasks, and each can be a little less hefty than if the other were not present. In addition, the cockpit rim, acting as an "L" flange, serves to further strengthen the deck.

In a similar case of interaction, it is clear that in a plywood-decked boat the breasthooks are backed up in their function by the deck itself, which acts as a large gusset. This means that they can be scaled back in length and thickness from the size they would have to be in an open boat.

Being aware of how their functions overlap will help you work out reasonable proportions between all the component parts. To recap, it's always worthwhile to examine a boat's parts in relation to their function. A rail meant to absorb horizontal forces may be made wider rather than deeper. Pieces resisting vertical stress may be thin and deep. A rail meant to handle abrasion as well as stress may need to be sized quite a bit larger than otherwise called for, and be made from an altogether different material as well, say oak instead of spruce.

Typical scantlings for several boats appear here. Although "correct," they should not be taken as the last or only word on the subject. Use them as a starting point in your own research and development in the field. Although it is a small consolation at the time, sometimes mistakes are the best teachers of all, and only through making something wrong—and discovering this under field conditions—do we begin to see what is right.

11-FOOT SOLO CANOE

Planks	4 millimeter
Rail (girder)	½ inch depth × ⁹⁄₁₆ inch width; blocks ½ inch depth × ¼ inch width × 4 inches
Keel, Sitka spruce	⅝ inch × 1¼ inches, tapered at ends (fiberglass tape may be substituted for keel)
Stem, laminated spruce	½ inch × ¾ inch, 8-10 laminae (fiberglass tape may be substituted)
Breasthook	⅝ inch thick, about 4½ inches on sides

A 16-FOOT CANOE

Planks	4 millimeter
Rail (girder)	⅝ inch width × ⁹⁄₁₆ inch depth; blocks ⁹⁄₁₆ inch depth × ⁵⁄₁₆ inch width × 5 inches
Keel	⅝ inch × 2 inches, tapered at ends (fiberglass tape may be substituted)
Stem	¾ inch × 1⅛ inches as above (fiberglass tape may be substituted)
Breasthooks	¾ inch thick arms, about 5 to 6 inches on a side

16- TO 18-FOOT KAYAK

Planks	4 millimeter
Inwale	⅝ inch depth × ⁹⁄₃₂ inch width
Rubrail	½ inch depth × ¼ inch width, tapered at ends
Keel	⅝ inch depth × 1 inch width spruce (fiberglass tape may be substituted)
Stems	⅞-inch spruce board (fiberglass tape may be substituted)
Cockpit rim	laminate of Honduras mahogany—about 5 laminae, total thickness about ¼ to ⁵⁄₁₆ inch, or a flat, laminated rim made of plywood, about ½ inch thick
Deckbeam	Spruce laminate, about 1 to 1¼ inches depth, ½ to ⅝ inches width

7. The Building Form

ithout some way to give them form, planks are just flat assemblies of wood. The way we get the correct form and give our boats their three-dimensional shape is by using a building form, or jig. This consists of the molds, which are sections of the hull cut from plywood, properly spaced apart on a common centerline, and erected on a foundation or platform. This chapter deals step by step with how to set up a form for the boats in this book.

Molds

The molds are, in essence, a special class of patterns, each mold representing the cross-sectional shape of the boat at a station along the boat's length. They can be made out of ¾-inch stock. Plywood is a good choice but somewhat hard to bevel. Natural wood, preferably pine, can be used but will require more work to make.

When building plywood station molds (hereafter called sections), you can use the factory edge of the plywood for a baseline, so that the mold can sit directly on the building platform. The height of the boat's

Figure 7-1. Drawing a mold full size. The 11-foot canoe's midsection mold is shown here. Plywood of ⅝- or ¾-inch thickness is suitable. A factory edge serves as the baseline and rests directly on the box or strongback. The centerline and the "waterlines," which connect the chine points, are shown here. The distance A will vary with each mold, and is obtained from the table of offsets. (For the canoe midsection, it is 10.37 inches.) The distance B is a half-breadth, 11.84 inches in this instance. This mold is drawn for building upside down. The shaded excess is cut off after the layout is complete.

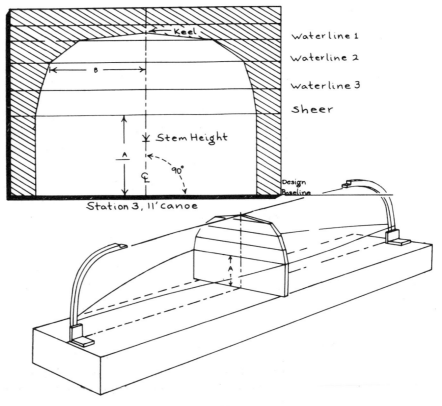

sheer above the baseline (keeping in mind that we are building upside down) will vary with each section, and is obtainable from the offsets.

Starting from the baseline, erect a perpendicular centerline on each mold. Now draw a line parallel to the centerline at a distance just a little greater than the greatest halfbreadth on both the right and left sides of the centerline. You can measure up these lines to find the ends of your horizontal reference lines (the heights above base in the offsets). Draw a line between each resultant pair of points using a pencil and a straight-edge, and you will have a series of horizontal lines parallel to the baseline. I call these waterlines, although they are not waterlines by strict definition. Rather, they denote the proper heights above the base on which to locate the chine points.

To locate each chine point, measure out from the centerline on the appropriate waterline the halfbreadth given in the table of offsets. When this process is completed on both the right and left sides of each water-line, connect all the points and the mold is drawn.

The horizontal line that connects the two sheer points is a good reference for erecting and checking the molds during setup. For this reason it is good to draw the sheer reference line and the centerline on both faces of the mold, but it is not necessary to draw the other points on both faces.

Another reason I like to connect all the chine points with horizontal lines is so that I can relocate them at the right height if the endpoints are lost in beveling, which happens easily enough.

Mold Setup

We have touched on the fact that the molds are sections of the hull drawn full-sized and come to life in the form of plywood shapes. They are the temporary building forms that define the shape over which we will fasten the planks, and you probably can visualize that they are somehow strung out along a centerline to make the building jig, although the details may not be completely clear in your mind.

The details of the building mold are on the drawing of the boat and in the offsets. These tell you how many stations there are, how far apart they are spaced, and the height above the baseline of a given reference point on each mold. Since it is easiest to build these boats upside down, the most convenient reference height to use is the height of the sheer above the baseline.

There are several ways to set up the molds—that is, to physically arrange and secure the stations in place. We will consider two: the ladder and the box.

The Ladder

The ladder is essentially what its name implies, a frame of two 2 × 4s, 2 × 6s, or 2 × 8s held together on edge and parallel to one another by

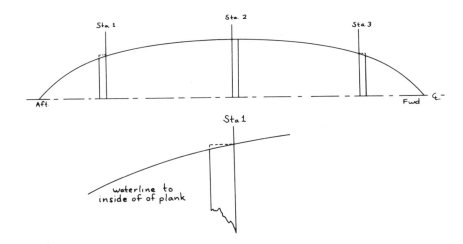

Figure 7-2. Placement of molds on the station lines. The molds are set forward or aft of the station lines, as appropriate, to leave some "meat" in the mold edge for beveling. Here the mold thicknesses are exaggerated for effect. The mold on station 2 could be either forward or aft of its station line, or centered on it, since it will be nearly square-edged.

cross-spalls (2 × 4 is a good size for these). A good ladder width for a canoe or kayak might be somewhere near the maximum beam of the boat. For added rigidity you may want to fasten a pair of spalls across the ends of the ladder, and plywood gussets as well, to make it more of a box and less likely to wrack.

The cross-spalls are fastened on the flat, perpendicular to the run of the ladder. Each spall forward of the longitudinal centerpoint of the boat needs to be placed so that its forward edge is perfectly aligned with the station line. In other words, the molds in the forward half of the boat sit in front of the stations, which means the cross-spalls must sit behind the stations.

In the after sections just the opposite is true. The molds are set behind the station lines, with the spalls in front of them. This ensures that the mold edges protrude enough to accept bevels for the plank landings. Figure 7-2 makes this clear.

The easiest, best way to fasten the cross-spalls is with sheetrock screws and either a screw gun or a driver bit in an electric drill.

In fact, sheetrock screws are the quickest, best way to do all your setup work. Screws are fast, positive fasteners, and they can be moved if something needs to be changed. They do not jar or move the work the way driving a nail might. You may need to drill a pilot hole so the screws don't split light bracing, but they are self-starting, self-tapping, and self-countersinking.

I like to use clamps to hold everything in place while I doublecheck the setup. If all is well I drive the screws. Another approach is to use one screw to hold an assembly temporarily, then drive a second screw to lock everything down when you're satisfied that the alignment is correct.

The ladder has a centerline strung or snapped onto it as the main reference from which all halfbreadths (or widths) are measured. A snapped chalkline is good, but pencil it in so it doesn't get rubbed off. A string or better still a fine wire stretched along the ladder is an even better centerline. The tops of the cross-spalls describe a horizontal plane that

Figure 7-3. A completed ladder-frame strongback with a mold erected.

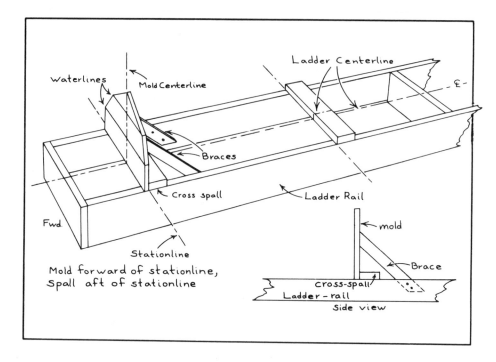

serves as the baseline. One disadvantage of the ladder is that the baseline is indeterminate between cross-spalls, but since almost all the measuring takes place at the molds, which are fastened to the cross-spalls, this is not an overriding problem.

If it is made sturdy enough not to wrack (and this is simply enough accomplished with strategically placed plywood gussets), the ladder has the virtue of being "self referential." This means that the molds are set perpendicular to the ladder baseline and square to its centerline, which may be level and plumb with the world but need not be so. Thus the ladder can be moved from place to place and still be used; even if it isn't level, it will be true to itself.

The Box

My personal favorite way to set up, and the one I recommend, is to use a plywood box as the foundation for the molds. The box is the most stable, rigid platform I've seen for the molds, and it provides excellent nailing or screwing for any necessary bracing. It is well suited to be self-referential, and the top of the box offers a continuous baseline plane, available wherever needed. I like to use a piano wire centerline for improved accuracy.

In building the box it is important to stagger the joints to prevent any tendency to sag, or the baseline/top will be rendered useless. See Figure 7-4 for ideas.

I have found that for the boats in this book a box about 13 to 14 inches wide and the same depth is good. One factor is how efficiently I

Figure 7-4. A box-platform strongback for molds, showing how to distribute joints to avoid sagging. This 12-foot box, made from 8-foot sheets of ¾-inch plywood, is suitable for building the 11-foot canoe and the 16-foot kayak. Use both glue and screws for sturdy construction.

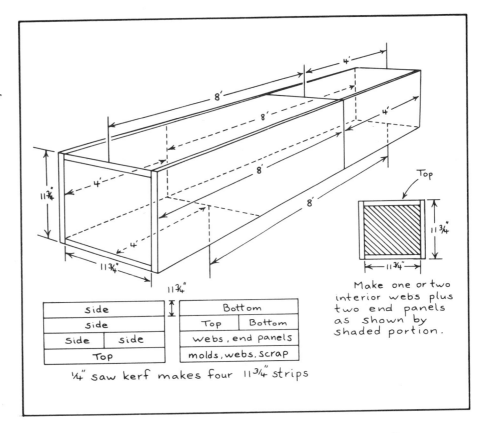

side	
side	
side	side
Top	

Bottom	
Top	Bottom
webs, end panels	
molds, webs, scrap	

¼" saw kerf makes four 11¾" strips

Make one or two interior webs plus two end panels as shown by shaded portion.

can cut up the plywood to maximize the depth without needing an extra sheet. The depth is the most important dimension for resistance to sag, but width is important in that too narrow a box will be unstable, especially when the molds are loaded down with clamps. If at all possible get the plywood for the box ripped to size on a table saw so that the edges are straight and all pieces are the same width. Failing that, use a straight-edged piece of lumber to guide your saw and do the best you can. The box is closed at each end and has a center web or bulkhead to aid in its stiffness and strength.

You will still need cross-spalls for fastening the molds; 2 × 4s fastened on the flat do very well. The comments on placement (under "The Ladder," above) apply here as well.

Erecting the Molds

Having chosen a suitable foundation, we can begin the actual setting up of the molds. This calls for patience and accuracy but is straightforward work.

I like to begin with the center mold and work forward and aft from there, but there is no reason why you couldn't start at one end and work your way through to the other.

With a ladder frame you need to lay out the station lines when you

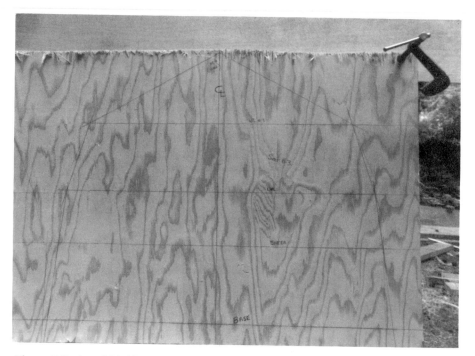

Figure 7-5. A mold laid out on ¾-inch plywood before cutting out. The centerline, baseline, and chine line markings are visible. Note that the horizontal lines are drawn from one side of the mold to the other so they can be used as reference lines when setting up and so that if the point they describe is lost, the line is still there to aid in reestablishing it. It will be helpful to draw the vertical centerline on both faces of the mold for setup purposes. To align, set the mold centerline over the box centerline, and fasten. Some small amount of fine-tuning may be needed to make sure the mold is square to the box centerline. Small shims or wedges between the mold and the cross-spall should do the trick for this. Check mold height from the offsets and use shims or wedges to adjust this as needed.

fasten the cross-spalls, so we can assume that your ladder already has the station lines on it. With a box you do better to lay out the station lines after the box is built; we will assume that the lines are drawn and the cross-spalls are now in place.

If you are using a wire centerline you will need to raise it just off the baseline plane. I use small scraps of brass about ³⁄₃₂ inch thick and tighten the wire with a piano tuning pin. You could probably improvise something like a tuning pin out of a woodscrew or lag bolt, drilling the shank to accept the wire. You will need to notch the molds around the wire, but that is easy enough to do. Notch the cross-spalls, too, if you're building on a box, so you won't have to raise the wire centerline above them.

Set the molds on the correct edge of the cross-spall with the centerline of the mold right over the mold centerline. If you have notched around the wire, then extend the mold centerline down to the wire with a straightedge to check the alignment. If you have used the factory edge

Figure 7-6. A cross-spall, to which a station mold will be screwed. Note station line on box. Spalls forward of the midstation are placed aft of the layout line; spalls aft of the centerline are forward of the layout line. This is so the molds themselves can be correctly placed. Forward molds are positioned with their aft face right on the layout line and the body of the mold forward of it, to allow for beveling. Aft molds have their forward faces on the layout line and the body of the mold aft of it. The cross-spall positions the mold at the correct fore-and-aft location and serves as a foundation to hold it, since the mold is fastened to it with sheetrock screws. The box centerline can also just be made out.

of the plywood as the mold baseline, chances are good that the mold is now exactly where you want it. You may want to doublecheck the sheer height above the baseline, however, by measuring it on both sides. If it needs adjustment, small shims can be slipped under the mold. Now clamp the mold to the cross-spall and use two or more screws to fasten it. Repeat the procedure on all the molds.

Having got the molds properly centered and at the right height, I use a plastic draftsman's triangle to be sure that the center mold is perpendicular to the top of the box or the horizontal reference plane. When it is right I brace it into position. Getting this correct may take some doing, and clamps or an extra pair of hands can be useful. I precut the braces (it is easy to estimate their size since the mold is nearly perpendicular already) and fasten them to the mold—usually by screwing through the plywood into the brace. Then I can lightly clamp the brace to the box or ladder and move it by gentle hammer taps until the mold is right, using more screws to complete the job.

Figure 7-7. The 'midship mold is the only one that needs to be braced; the others can be held in relation to it. Note the use of a plastic drafting triangle to ensure that the mold is perpendicular to the strongback surface. "Horning in" (see Figure 7-8) assures that it is set correctly athwartships. Braces are attached by screws driven through from the opposite face of the mold. The braces are fastened to the mold first, then the assembly is plumbed and aligned, and finally the other ends of the braces are screwed to the box to anchor everything.

The height of the mold is given in the offsets. Since this boat is being built upside down, the relevant information is the height of the sheer above the baseline. For ease, the baseline is taken as the top of the box, and the mold is cut out with the correct margin of plywood so that when its bottom surface is on the box the sheer is the right height above it.

Before fastening everything down, check the squareness of the molds to the centerline. The best way to do this is by measurement— what the old-timers called "horning in."

Drive a small brad in the centerline a good distance away from the mold. Hook your steel tape over this and measure to one edge of the station mold at a known height above the baseline. The sheer point is probably the best ready reference to use. Now measure over to the sheer point on the other side of the mold. If the measurements are the same, the mold is square. If not, force small wedges or shims between the mold and the cross-spall until the measurements match. The longer the side of the triangle that you measure, the more accurate the method will be, so drive in the brad as far from the mold as possible.

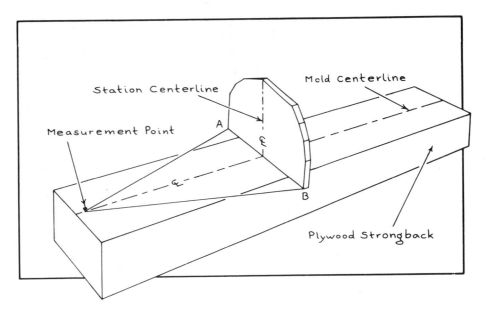

Figure 7-8. Setting the center mold square to the strongback centerline, a process known as horning in. Only the midstation need be horned in; the others may be set square with reference to that one. A brad to serve as a hook for a steel tape makes a good measurement point on the centerline. The longer the measurements from there to points A and B, the more accurate the setup. When leg A equals leg B, the mold is square. The sheer points are convenient choices for A and B.

Once one mold is plumbed, squared, and braced, it is simple enough to set the others in relation to it, especially since these boats don't use many molds. I prefer the center mold as a master reference for the others, since its central location and greatest width makes it the easiest to brace strongly.

False Stems

Taped seam construction allows you to skip the use of conventional keels and stems if you wish. Although this will call for a little more taping and filleting, it avoids the problems of laminating stems, attaching them to keels, and beveling these members.

If you elect not to use them there is one problem to overcome. Sighting against an actual stem is a big help in the lining out and planking of a boat. Even though plank measurements are provided for the 11-foot canoe and 16-foot kayak, it is a real aid and an aesthetically sound idea to have an actual stem (or stern) profile to work to.

I have found that I can make up false stems to slide in and out of the mold in such a way that I can use them as aids in the planking yet not include them in the structure of the boat. Nor do they require anything

Figure 7-9. Removable canoe stem pattern with penciled-in plank lines—a useful mechanical and conceptual aid while building. (Not part of the finished boat.) Can be used to position and check planks, slid out of the way for taping, etc., slid back for next plank, and so forth.

Figure 7-10. Detail of the stem pattern on the mold. It can be slid into position along the slot.

Figure 7-11. *The stem pattern is tightly held at the strongback by two blocks tapered to miss the planking. It can be slid in this simple track for fore-and-aft adjustment or lifted out as need be.*

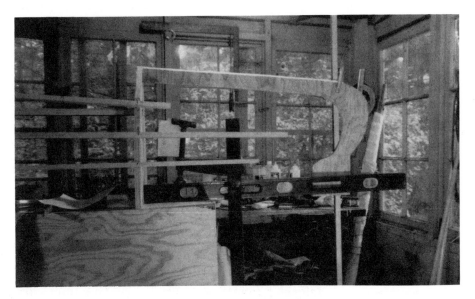

Figure 7-12. *A kayak stem pattern. This false stem is removable as in Figure 7-9, but in this case the boat is longer than the strongback. The 4-foot level is being used as a straightedge only to extend the baseline (the top of the strongback box). A predrawn line on the stem, gotten from the plans, marks where this plane (at the bottom of the level) should intersect the stem. The inboard end of the stem piece is notched into the end mold as in Figure 7-10, and the outboard end is held by a strut. A temporary shore and a clamp are used to hold the stem at the right height.*

Figure 7-13. Detail of Figure 7-12. The strut that holds the stem piece has been added. This strut is offset half the thickness of the stem from the longitudinal centerline of the boat. In other words, the strut is placed far enough off the centerline so that the stem centerline is right over the mold centerline. The amount of offset depends on the thickness of the stem. In this case, with a ⅝-inch plywood stem, the inside face of the strut (away from camera) is ⁵⁄₁₆ inch from the mold centerline and parallel to it.

but the most cursory and rough beveling, with no premium being placed on careful or accurate work. It is just a matter of working the square edge of the plywood stem form down to an angle—any angle—that won't interfere with the planks coming together. If you elect to use a false stem, the accompanying pictures tell the story more clearly than words can. I find that false stems are most effective if left in place while I plank the whole boat, thus giving me the most control and visual reinforcement. They are then removed, and the taping process is begun. I recommend this approach for your first one or two boats, and used it for the boats photographed in this book.

Once all the molds have been set up, you'll want to tack a batten through the chine points at each waterline, clamping it to the false stem at the appropriate waterline mark and letting it extend a little beyond the stem. It doesn't matter which side of the chine you run the batten, as long as you're consistent. Then step back from your work and view the batten from several angles. If an abrupt bump or hollow is evident in an otherwise smooth sweep, pull the tack from the offending mold and let the batten assume a fair curve. If it springs free of the mold edge, you'll

Figure 7-14. Same stem seen from the other side. Two screws and the notch are all that is needed to hold everything in place. Also showing are the battens I used to line off the planking. Because the plank shapes for the 11-foot canoe and the 16-foot kayak are provided in this book, you won't have to line off this carefully, but I still recommend you do some batten work to test for a fair sweep along the chine points at each waterline, and as discussed in Chapter 10, I recommend use of a batten when cutting the planks to their final shapes.

Figure 7-15. A false piece for the stern of the kayak. Whereas the stem piece (Figure 7-12) was deep enough to connect directly with the strut, here a scrap of plywood is added to do the job. This creates an additional offset factor to figure in. Graphically drawing out such an arrangement is a good way to figure out what's needed, and it's a little safer than mental gymnastics.

Figure 7-16. Overall setup for the 11-foot canoe. Three-quarter-inch plywood box, about 12 inches square, used as strongback and mold platform. Diagonal bracing on center mold; other molds braced to center mold with 1 × 3 struts. Molds are fastened to 2 × 4 cross-spalls that are fastened with sheetrock screws precisely on the mold lines. Holes in one edge of the mold accommodate clamps, useful when lining out.

have to pad out the missing plank land with a wedge. If the batten springs inside the existing chine line, you need only make a mark and plane off the excess material from the mold edge. Be careful though. Sometimes the position of the batten ends can make a good mold setup seem unfair. A light shift of a batten end may remove a bump or hollow elsewhere, and is the first thing to try. A batten that is about 2 feet longer than the setup at each end minimizes this problem.

Beveling the Molds

The molds need to be beveled so that the planks will lie fairly across them when they are bent around the jig. If they were square-edged, most of the edge would be outside the fair curve of the hull as seen from above and would create a hard corner for the plank to bend around, thus kinking or distorting the lay of the plank. Figure 7-2 shows this clearly.

With all its mystery removed, beveling is just the process of knocking down those high corners so the plank can lie in the plane it is meant to assume.

Figure 7-17. Two overall views (bow right) of a kayak-building setup with planks lined off. Only the center mold is braced, the others being held in place by 1 × 3s and battens. Note how the forward frames are forward of the station lines and aft frames are aft of the station lines, to leave meat for beveling.

In normal ribbed construction the planks need to fit tightly to the ribs, and accurate beveling is a must. Since that constraint is not present for us, the demands on the beveling are not as great. The mold serves to position and anchor the plank until the seams are taped, but the absolute need for "glue-joint quality" over the entire mold edge is just not there.

Without advocating sloppiness, shoddiness, and gross dereliction of duty, I can say that you may safely relax a bit while beveling. As long as there is enough contact to fasten the plank without distorting it, and as long as the plank is lying where it should, it doesn't matter if the bevel

Figure 7-18. A close-up of the kayak's 'midships mold. Note cross-spalls, bracing, and 1 × 3s to connect other molds. The uppermost batten marks the keel centerline, as a check for a fair sweep.

isn't precisely right over its full width or length, or if it goes off the mark here and there.

Except on slab-sided boats, the bevel of the molds will change from sheer to keel. The bevel almost always is least at the sheer, so if, when you cut out the molds, you cut to the angle given for the sheer you will be safe, only needing to deepen it by hand on the other parts as needed. On the drawings of the canoe and kayak in this book the mold edge bevels at the sheer are given in degrees, or more precisely, the number of degrees out of square.

In order to cut bevels properly, you need to have an accurate means of measuring and transferring angles. Boatbuilding bevel gauges, which are smaller than the ordinary cabinetmaker's variety, are commercially available, but they are also easy enough to make yourself. I use little scraps of maple or some other hardwood for the body, and an old hacksaw blade for the blade. A copper rivet makes a fine pivot. Don't forget to grind the teeth off the hacksaw! And be sure the two edges of the blade are parallel.

Having said all that, I hasten to add that it is equally feasible to cut the molds out square-edged and then bevel them once the jig is set up. Frankly I have found that this is probably the easier method. The square edges are easier to cut and somewhat more convenient to use during setup, and it is much easier to keep the chine lines this way.

After the molds have been set up on the box or ladder, it is easy enough to bend a batten around them and check the bevels. The batten will show the angle you need at each chine, and it will show what side of the edge is high and needs to come off. You can use the batten as an indicator and spot-bevel a small patch under it using a rasp. Then enlarge this spot to cover the whole plank land that you are working on. (A plank land for these boats is the area between two chines, defining where a plank will lie.) Do this on each mold until the batten is lying fairly and in even contact with all mold edges.

As discussed in Chapter 10, I feel that the easiest way to mark a plank for final cutting is to lay it in position over the molds, with a batten temporarily tacked across the molds at the appropriate chine. In this instance, I use a four-penny finish nail driven through the batten and into the mold to hold the batten in place. You can use this nail as a peg and remove and reset the batten in the same nail hole. If it feels a little loose, just give the nail a few more taps. When spot-checking bevels as described above, I usually hold the batten in place with my hands (this lets me slide it around to check the whole plank land), but if I need a nail I use one here too.

Assuming you are building with a false stem and stern, you will need to set up and run the batten through these points as well.

For the actual beveling a rasp is a good tool to begin with, as mentioned, just to establish a spot with the right bevel. Then a sharp block plane or the scrub plane can come into play. If a lot of material has to come off, a scrub plane or fishtail gouge is excellent. An electric plane is also a good tool for beveling, and, depending on how deeply it is set, can be used either for hogging or fine-tuning. The electric plane is particularly good for plywood, but watch for tear-out on the ends. Using the rotation of the cutter to cut toward the meat of the mold rather than toward the end is the way to minimize this problem.

In addition to the full-length batten that you use to spot the bevels, a wider batten (to simulate the plank) is good to use for intermediate checking. The longer this batten is, the better. It should be long enough to span at least three molds—one mold either side of the mold you are checking.

The secret to successful beveling is to be bold at first, when there is a lot of removal needed, and then to slow down as you get closer to the final surface. Check frequently with the wide batten so you aren't working in the dark. The best final arbiter is the plank itself, and you should fine-tune the bevels with that in place if there is any question.

The Optional Backbone

Traditional construction called for a backbone—keel, ribs, stem, sternpost, and so forth. This was the framework that served as a foundation for the planking. As we have seen, in glued and taped construction these structures are optional.

BEVEL TIPS

Beveling is sometimes a stumbling block for the beginning boatbuilder. Plan ahead, work slowly, and check your work frequently—even every few shavings if it's a critical spot. You can't just blindly plane away at a piece and hope that it will all come out right. You need to see how much material you are removing, where it is being taken from, and how much more remains.

Making accurate bevels and good fits isn't difficult if you follow a systematic procedure. Obviously, you'll "measure twice to cut once," but you'll also need to accurately determine the correct bevels and then lay them out on the workpiece. Careful layout and precise measurement are essential before you cut.

A "rough cut" means sawing to the line as closely as you can, leaving it showing as a reference and as "insurance." Don't go inside the line, whatever you do. On the other hand, if you leave too much, you are liable to lose your hard-won bevels just getting down to the line.

When sawing a bevel, an obvious but often overlooked point is the importance of clamping your work firmly. You're doomed to failure if you try to saw accurately on a vibrating, sliding piece.

When you have cut to the line, fit the work exactly in place and look at it. Are the bevels nearly right? Is the size correct? If so, you may only need to smooth off the saw cut with a plane to get your final fit.

If the bevel is wrong, use pencil marks on the part of the edge that needs to come off. When the pencil marks disappear, you know that you are cutting in the right place. Watch your work by looking right through the throat of the plane to see where the cut is taking place. Let the width and placement of the shaving guide you. Clear the throat as needed to keep track.

Often the hardest part is holding the plane at the right angle. It's easy to have it roll onto the wrong bevel, particularly when planing the thin edge of a board or plank. It helps to use a low grip on the plane, with the hands low on the body and the thumb and fingers cradling the handles rather than gripping them.

If a bevel is getting too rounded and you're becoming frustrated, sometimes a change of tools may be in order. If the plane seems to be the culprit, try a different one, or use a chisel or rasp instead.

Are you using the right plane? On a curved or irregular surface, a plane that is too long will not be able to get down into every hollow, or it may just catch the apex of the curve. Skewing the plane effectively shortens the sole and is an easy way to get into small hollows without changing planes. Sometimes, though, you will need a spokeshave because even a few inches of sole is too long.

In a changing bevel, a longer plane may not work because part of the sole is still riding on the old bevel and consequently isn't able to react to the new angle. This happens at the forefoot of my solo canoes in keel beveling (when I choose to incorporate a keel) and makes it necessary to use spokeshaves and a rasp for a 9-inch section.

If you have a rounded bevel you can't tame with a plane, try using a sharp paring chisel to bring down the high areas. This is especially effective if just the center of the bevel is affected and the edges need to be left alone. Another way to attack this particular problem is to use a rasp, which can give more selective control of the cut in some situations. Use a diagonal, slicing motion.

If you're having problems, always be ready to suspect that your trouble stems from dull tools. Dulling has a way of affecting the performance of a tool so gradually that you may not be aware of it. Plywood is a favorite mold material, but it dulls tools quickly. Waiting too long to resharpen not only makes your work harder, but makes sharpening more work when you finally get around to it.

Look at the edges of your tools and test them frequently. A dull edge will show a line of reflection, but a true knife edge will not reflect light. When in doubt, hone. Use a whetstone (I like the Japanese water-stones) to hone a slightly dulled edge; use a grinding wheel to condition badly dulled and chipped edges before final honing with a whetstone.

There are a number of ways of checking your bevels. The best arbiter of a mold edge or stem bevel will be the plank itself; if it lies on the molds nicely, your bevels are right. If you don't have a roughed-out plank ready, you can use a batten. Try to use a batten that is as similar to the actual piece as possible in width, thickness, and bendability, so it will behave as much like the plank as possible. If there is a lot of twist or a quick change in the bevel, this will be the only way you have to be sure you have the bevel right.

I think that ribless construction is the greatest thing to happen to boats in years. For maximizing interior volume, and for cleaning and maintenance, leaving out the ribs is the best thing you can do.

Keels and stems, on the other hand, make nice references when setting up a mold. They give a tangible centerline to work toward. For some builders, myself included, having the planks meet on a stem rather than just coming together in mid air is easier to deal with—if only conceptually. The keel is also a good place to put your foot when entering or leaving a boat, much more satisfactory than stepping onto the light planking, even if it is supported by the water. It's the best place to put a builder's plate, if that appeals to you, and can serve as a good landing for a mast step where that applies.

The scantling information in Chapter 6 will guide you in determining sizing for a stempiece or keel, should you decide to include them. Transfer shape information from the measured drawings.

Including these members may add some more weight and cause more work. You'll need to notch the keel into the molds (see Figure 7-19), and it will need to be beveled for planking. The stem—both bow and stern in a double-ender—will need to be laminated (Figure 7-20) and then attached to the keel. In light work such as this, a glue joint alone is sufficient. A simple half-lap (Figure 7-21) seems to work quite well. This method is simple, but requires accuracy; the stems need to be straight and true in relation to the keel centerline. I begin by aligning the penciled-in keel and stem centerlines, and doublecheck by horning-in.

The stems also require beveling for the planking, and some means of securing them to the mold in the correct position. The clamping is tricky.

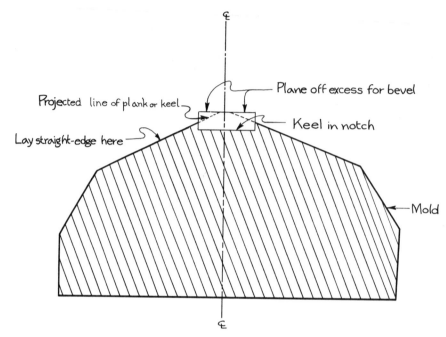

Figure 7-19. *The optional keel, if you decide to include it, needs to be notched into the molds. Lay out the notch and cut it into the mold with a backsaw and a chisel. If the keel is ½ to ⅝ inch thick, setting it into the mold about ¼ inch leaves enough meat for beveling. Running a straightedge along the garboard plank and letting it butt into the keel will show you exactly where the keel and plank intersect, and therefore how much bevel you will have. Ideally the straightedge should want to pass right through the centerline of the keel. If it wants to come out on the far side of the centerline you are beveling off too much material, and the keel needs to be set a little deeper in the molds. I fasten the keel to the mold with a single sheetrock screw. Drill a pilot hole to avoid splitting something. Be careful that the bottom of the notch is flat and level and that the keel is held so it isn't canted to one side or the other. If it is, use thin shims to level it athwartships. It usually isn't necessary to use a screw at every station; use just enough to hold the keel snugly on the right curve, without rocking.*

Figure 7-20. *A laminating form for an optional canoe stem, the shape for which is obtained from the lines plan and offsets. It is made of three layers of ¾-inch plywood, with holes cut to give the clamps purchase. The first two layers are cut precisely to the stem shape, while the back layer is cut oversize to serve as a fence, which is essential in keeping the laminae aligned and stacked one over another. A thin strip has been "clamped" into place to show the way it is used. The entire form is waxed before every use to prevent glue from bonding to it. Epoxy glue is used in the lamination. When the laminating is complete, the ends are sawn so that, initially, the stem stands a bit above the sheer. Later, after the breasthook is fitted, the stem is sawn flush and the whole structure faired to a smoothly flowing, pleasing form. For more information on building a laminated part, see the section on laminating cockpit rims in Chapter 12.*

Figure 7-21. The optional backbone: Attaching a laminated canoe stem to the keel with a half-lap joint. A 1½- to 3-inch overlap is sufficient; longer is okay.

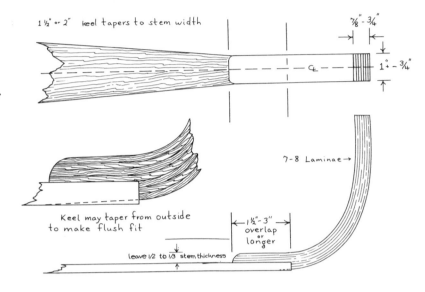

1½" or 2" keel tapers to stem width

⅞"-¾"

1"-¾"

₵

7-8 Laminae →

Keel may taper from outside to make flush fit

1½"-3" overlap or longer

leave 1/2 to 1/3 stem thickness

Figure 7-22. The optional backbone: Using a bracket to hold the stem for fastening. The stem centerline should be plumbed over the strongback centerline, and the bracket must be offset enough to permit this. A ¼-inch bolt with wingnut holds the stem to the bracket, which is well clear of the sheerline so as not to interfere with planking. The stem end need not sit directly on the box.

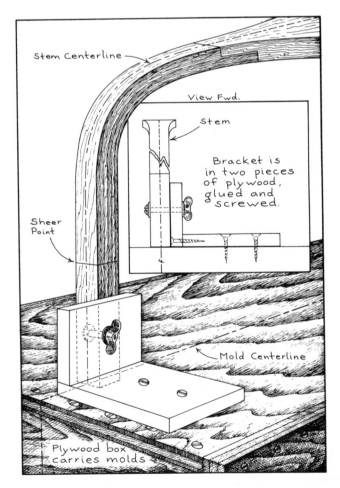

Stem Centerline

View Fwd.

Stem

Bracket is in two pieces of plywood, glued and screwed.

Sheer Point

Mold Centerline

Plywood box carries molds

In light of all this you may be tempted to skip the backbone, and, as mentioned, I recommend this for the first boat you build.

If you do elect to eliminate the physical structure of the stem and keel, you will still need a functional equivalent, something to join the planks where they meet. The usual substitute is a seam made with fiberglass tape. The job of filleting and taping these joints can be messy, frustrating work, especially at the stem. It is not easy, in my opinion, to get a

Figure 7-23. The optional backbone: Using a series of points, or "spot bevels," to rough in a rapidly changing bevel on a canoe stem. The proper bevel at each spot is most easily obtained using a batten over the molds. For light work such as this the bevel could be cut with a rasp or paring chisel. The spots are then faired together in one smooth curve with a block plane, rasp, etc.

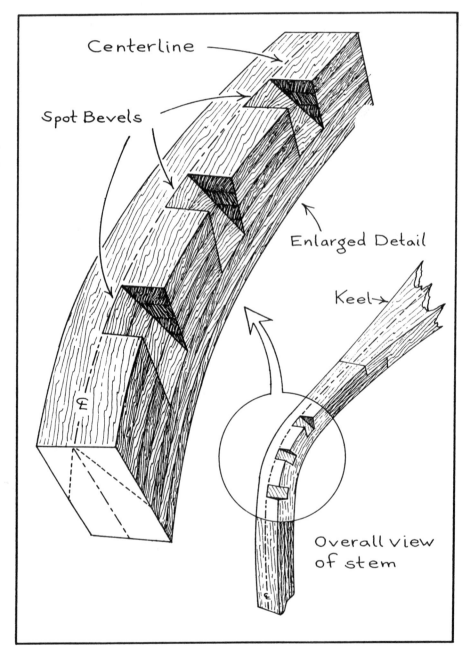

really finished look to taped seams, and extra care at this juncture will pay aesthetic dividends.

As mentioned earlier, temporary stem and stern patterns, their shapes transferred from the drawings, are useful aids when it's time to join the planking at the ends of the boat.

If you decide in favor of the backbone, use light screws to hold the keel in place on the molds. Remember to notch the garboards around the screws so that you can back them out when you take the hull off the mold. The garboard notches can later be filled and faired with epoxy, but you will probably want to whittle tight-fitting plugs for the screw holes in the keel.

To hold a permanent stem for fastening, I use an angle bracket made of a 2 × 3 that I have planed or otherwise machined to a true right angle. The short leg of the angle fastens to the mold, and the other leg holds the stem. I position the angle block so that it holds the stem centerline directly over the mold centerline, and I use a stop block to keep the stem in the correct fore-and-aft position as well. I use a ¼-inch machine screw and a wingnut to hold the stem to the post. The entire system is fast and accurate.

Make up your stems longer than the finished size so you will have some extra length to work with. It's also a good idea to have the stem-holding jig below the sheerline so that it doesn't get in the way of clamping or any other plank hanging operations.

A critical point is that the angle block be fastened perpendicular to the mold's horizontal reference so there is no lean or skew in the stem. You may need to use wedges or shims under the block to achieve this.

The backbone, like the mold itself, will need to be beveled for the planking. Keel bevels can be taken from the molds at the stations. Stem bevels are best gotten with a batten, or better still with an oversized, roughed-in plank blank. The techniques and comments from the mold-beveling section may apply here as well.

Once you are satisfied with the bevels, wax the mold so that no glue will stick to it while you do the preliminary taping. I use regular Butcher's Wax. Put on several coats since the end-grain of the plywood will soak it up.

With all this mold and (possibly) backbone work done—and it may have seemed like a long time in coming—you are finally ready to start planking the boat.

8. Fastening, Clamping, and Gluing

Fastening, clamping, and gluing covers the art of making the pieces of the boat stay together once you have made them fit. Its importance cannot be overstressed, even if it appears to be less demanding of skill than some of the other, more romantic boatbuilding operations.

Wood can be nailed, screwed, riveted, and bolted. Not so long ago, even a small boat might have taken hundreds or even thousands of nails, tacks, and screws to knit its fabric into unity. In modern light construction with good joints and epoxy glue, you will find that glue joints alone are strong enough, although you may need to jog your mindset before you can really accept this truth. It took a real effort of will not to put any fasteners into my first glue-constructed boat. Fasteners still have their uses, however.

Fasteners

An obvious point is that fasteners should be the right size in relation to the piece they are fastening. It's almost equally bad to use too long or too short a screw or nail. Stress on a fastener is greatest right at the interface of materials and tapers off from there. Too short a fastener puts nearly all the holding power in the stress zone and is weak. Too long a fastener—apart from being more expensive—will be more trouble to drive and place and may weaken or crack the wood. Also, most of the screw will be beyond the stress zone and therefore doing very little work.

The general rule of thumb states that the length of a fastener should be about three times the thickness of the material that it is fastening. For most light work this means that you will need No. 4-gauge screws, or No. 6 at the biggest. For nails, about No. 14-gauge will be fine. In most cases, anything bigger will be far too heavy.

A predrilled pilot hole is essential—not only for ease of driving, but to protect the matrix material from undue stress, cracking, or splitting. The threads develop more holding power when they bite into a slightly undersized hole than when they are forced into a solid piece. The latter can result in dulling the threads, or in a crack or split that greatly reduces holding power.

These small-gauge screws can strip and break very easily, so a pilot hole is important for this reason as well. In softwoods, especially spruce, a drill may be overkill. I use a small, tapered triangular awl, which I push in and spin. This makes a good start without sacrificing too much holding power.

Although I have been talking about screws, I find that it is just as important to drill pilot holes for annular nails.

When driving nails into light wood, it's good practice to use a backing iron. The backing iron, which can be a chunk of lead or a splitting wedge, gives some inertia to the delicate boat you are fastening into and allows the nail to absorb the hammer's force. It can be separated from the wood by some padding for protection.

Copper rivets make excellent fasteners since they are comparatively cheap and are nearly the functional equivalent of a bolt, with the exception that they do not have the same kind of thread-controlled drawing-together power that bolts do. Some people like their appearance and some don't.

Bolts are unsurpassed when real strength is needed. They are also invaluable in pulling together parts that are otherwise difficult to snug up using clamps or other means. Small, light machine screws in bronze are commonly available in lengths up to 3 inches.

Some type of countersinking is required for the fastener head. If you are using a light, round-headed machine screw in soft wood, you should place a washer under the head as well as under the nut.

Placement of fasteners is an art. On many boats—particularly guideboats and lapstrake hulls—the fasteners form a major aesthetic element in the final appearance. Usually symmetry is strived for, even when, from an engineering point of view, an uneven spacing might make better sense, since stress is not evenly distributed throughout most constructions.

Developing a good eye will be of aid here, but it is entirely acceptable to use a layout line and a rule or dividers to get an even spacing. I have even resorted to a calculator to determine the correct spacing mathematically. A slight staggering of fasteners alternately above and below the layout line is a good way not to get all your rivets or screws into one line of grain.

Part and parcel with the tyranny of symmetry is the business of screw heads. Having the slots all line up in the same direction is a small touch that looks good, and this seems to carry an awful lot of weight with some people in their estimation of "craftsmanship."

Foresight is also called for. The best place for one fastener invariably seems to be the best place for another. If you are going to screw on both the deck of a kayak and the rubrail, you would do well to map out the distribution of fastenings before you begin. It can save a lot of headaches.

Such considerations, however, are more relevant to traditional construction than to the boats in this book. When you start with glued construction—especially if you are used to a more traditional approach—you may have a hard time resisting the urge to stick fasteners all over the boat, "just in case." But glue *is* strong and it does its job. Fasteners are used sparingly—indeed they may only be needed to attach mechanical parts.

A few other areas where fasteners may be in order (or at least not patently ridiculous) would be where the planking meets the stems, keels, or transoms, or to reinforce breasthooks. Sometimes you might want to fasten a rail with screws, either so it can be replaced later, or because clamping it is beyond reasonable achievement.

The use of fasteners as temporary clamps or to align or draw together difficult pieces is practical and valid. Such techniques can be lifesavers, but first you will want to weigh considerations such as "Can this fastener be hidden?" or "How would a fastener look here?" In general I try to keep the use of fasteners to a minimum in glued work, and try to hide them if they are used. This contributes to simplicity, aesthetic unity, and a feeling that I have satisfied the general principle of the thing.

Gluing

Good glue joints are stronger than the wood itself and are not that hard to achieve. For best results, there are three major areas that need attention—the fit, the glue itself, and the pressure applied to the joint.

The fit must be good or all that follows will be in vain. Glued surface area is the bottom line of getting strong glue joints, and surface area can't exist where the pieces aren't in contact. Despite epoxy's gap-filling properties, you will be wise to make your fits as good as you can—think thousandths of an inch, not sixteenths.

Gluing is like a surgical procedure. It requires planning and care. When it is your only fastener, there is no room for error. Always run through a dry assembly first, checking all fits. Make any gauge or alignment marks that you will need. If you're fastening, do your drilling now to avoid getting chips in the glue and into the joint. I like to clamp the dry assembly with almost all the clamps I'll be using when I actually glue. Then I position them along the boat as I remove them so they are all right at hand in the correct order for the glue-up.

The next area of concern is the glue itself. It should be the right one for the job, correctly applied under proper conditions—which means clean materials, the right temperature and humidity, with all the necessary cups, mixers, clamps, pads, and associated accessories right at hand.

There is a variety of glues available to the boatbuilder today. Epoxies will probably top the list as the strongest, most durable, most tenaciously bonding, most waterproof, most expensive, and most toxic. Epoxies come in many formulations and configurations. Some are relatively temperature and mix-ratio sensitive, while others allow a greater range. If a particular glue is too cold, for instance, it will not set up in the proper time, nor will it possess the proper strength. You must decide for yourself what is best suited to your workplace and habits. Do you have special mixing equipment and an environment over 70° F? Or do you do your mixing in plastic cups in one bay of a two-car garage? In terms of cost and convenience, it's worthwhile putting some thought into your choice of epoxy.

Some glues are quite thin, while others are much thicker. Again, the specific application will decide for you. When applying fiberglass cloth or coating plywood, the thinner resins are the only way to go. But on vertical joints the same thin resin will run out and starve the joint unless thickeners are added. Thin glue tends to be absorbed by the end-grain more easily, which will lead to starved joints if care isn't taken.

I use a thick, wide-temperature-and-mix-ratio glue for structural work and laminating, and a thin resin for coating and sheathing. It is possible to save money by buying one glue for all these purposes, thickening it as necessary, but I believe in starting with a glue more nearly formulated for the use at hand. I try to avoid mix-sensitive glues because, at least for me, pumps are a source of frustration and waste. I mix in plastic cups and use waxed paper wherever I don't want out-of-bounds glue joints. Surgical supply houses carry graduated disposable cups that are handy for glue mixing; for small amounts I find that using plastic picnic spoons is a good way to keep mixing ratios under control, using a level spoon as the unit of measure.

It is essential to work as cleanly and neatly with epoxy as you can. This will make your boat look better and make it easier to finish, but it's most important for reasons of safety.

Get disposable gloves from a medical supply house and use them. Use an organic vapor respirator. If you do get glue on yourself, immediately wash it off with warm water and soap. Don't use a solvent; that will only help your skin to absorb it better.

It's not good to be rushed when you're gluing. Go through any special problems in the dry assembly and work them out there. Don't assume that "it will all work out" unless you really know so from experience.

Apply glue to both sides of the joint, in a quantity so that a small amount of squeeze comes out of the joint when you clamp up. Any epoxy that dribbles out will be much easier to clean up before it sets completely. It smears horribly when fresh, but anything is better than dealing with hunks of set-up glue. It's ideal to catch it in mid-cure when it is rubbery. At that point, big globs can be lifted off neatly with a putty knife or chisel.

The last element in a good job is applying the right pressure to the glued joint. Try to get the pieces in contact using a slight positive pressure. If you need too much pressure to make good fits, then the fits probably aren't really good. The discussion of clamping that follows contains some tips on the most efficient ways to apply this pressure.

I do a final check of alignment, clamp pressure, squeeze-out, heat tents, and so forth before I leave the assembly to dry on its own. I've forestalled a couple of nightmares by this habit. It's no fun to redo a glue job—especially at the end of a long day—but it's even less fun to find your mistake after the epoxy has set up like iron.

Epoxy may be king in most of today's boatshops, but for one job at least I prefer the ordinary water-mixed brown glue that is labeled "water resistant." It is much easier, neater, and cleaner to set bungs in this glue. The person who has to remove your bungs for later repairs will bless you for your wisdom and foresight. I've used this "plastic resin glue" for rail and plank scarfs with no problem as well. I have also met airplane builders who use this glue in preference to epoxy because of its strength under high temperatures (approximately 180° F and up). Unless you decide to use countersunk and bunged screws in a rubrail, however, you won't have occasion to need it. For structural work on boats, epoxy is a safer choice.

Fillers

There is a variety of powders and agents that can be added to epoxy resin to alter its characteristics. Silica powder can be added to thin mixtures to thicken them and make them less likely to run out of vertical or overhead joints. It is also used—and abused—to increase the gap-filling qualities of epoxy. Finally, it can be used when a thicker mixture is wanted for making fillets. Glass or cotton fibers can be added to resin for the latter purpose, however, and may make a less brittle mixture.

Adding silica to resin to make a batch of gap-filling "mashed potatoes" isn't always the best way to go. It's better to work on getting tighter fits. The technique works within reason, but large masses of silica and glue seem to be rather more brittle than plain resin, and the thicker mixture has less and less wetting-out ability, which affects bond strength and so becomes self-defeating after a while.

Silica and resin sets up very hard indeed; if you use the mixture, be neat and clean it up before it sets. Failure to observe this precaution can make finishing time a real nightmare.

Silica dust is light and pervasive. Wear an adequate respirator while you handle and mix it. It's best added in small amounts rather than in one huge scoop. Mix it in well before adding more so you can keep tabs on how dry the mixture is becoming. This is good advice when mixing any additive.

Cotton fibers are a lighter-weight way to make a filleting compound. Add in small amounts, since the mixture has a way of becoming too dry all of a sudden.

Chopped glass fibers make a very strong, if somewhat heavy, fillet.

Microballoons—little hollow plastic spheres—can be added to glue when you want a lightweight, easily worked fairing putty. It is not intended to be used in structural glue-ups. It is easily sanded or worked with a Surform (something the others are not), as befits its role in fairing. If you have trouble fairing your boat prior to final finishing, microballoons in epoxy will probably provide the answer.

Clamping

The subject of clamps was already introduced in Chapter 5. A wide selection of clamps is ideal because no one clamp is perfect for every job.

Different lengths, weights, shapes, and throat sizes are like money in the bank when some nonstandard circumstance arises. And boatbuilding can be one nonstandard episode after another.

Clamps should have pressure pads under them. This not only protects the wood, but spreads the pressure more evenly, which is particularly important when using thin stock. The pads can be small wood or plywood blocks, or long battens or strips, depending on the application.

Specially shaped pads, known as cauls, are used on curved or irregular surfaces where a normal pad would not do, or even where clamps may not stick at all. Cauls must fit their mating surface perfectly or you run the risk of creating a void (Figure 8–1).

Sometimes you can extend the reach of a clamp by using a wooden bar that is under the screw but reaches out past the throat. This is particularly suited to planking and decking problems.

Even when a clamp has the throat to make the reach, sometimes it won't stick because of the extreme difference in angle between the anvil and the screw. You may be able to arrange a wedge under the anvil to alleviate this problem. Of course, you will need some way to anchor the wedge so it doesn't creep as pressure is applied. I've used a scrap of stick braced against something solid (like a bulkhead in the mold), a small clamp, or even a tiny brad barely driven through the wedge to help hold it in place.

A related technique is to use blocking to create a whole new surface at a different angle—one that is better aligned—for the anvil to sit on. I've spanned between ribbands with a 2 × 4 scrap to achieve this effect.

There are times when you are trying to get a clamp to stick on a sharp edge rather than on a surface. This could occur on a ribband or a stem, for example. The solution is to make a small block that has a V cut into it, letting the block span the edge and rest on the two legs of the angle that converge to make the edge. This is a powerful and useful technique.

Figure 8-1. Use of a caul, or shaped pressure pad, to apply even pressure on a surface—in this case a lamination glue-up—that would be hard to clamp by normal means.

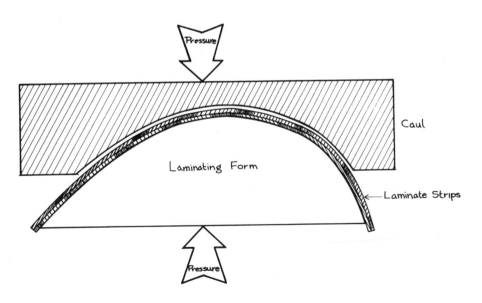

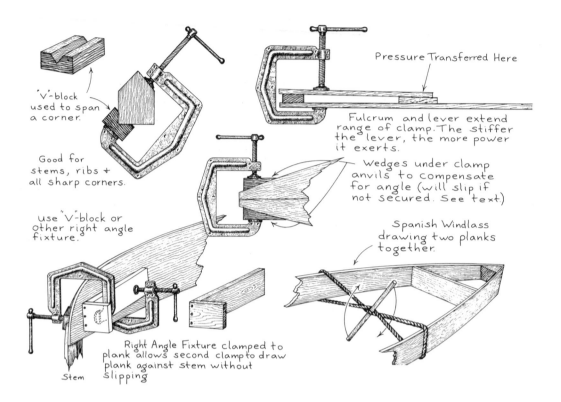

Figure 8-2. Nonstandard clamping procedures. Desperate times call for desperate measures.

Trying to clamp the converging sides of a triangle can cause lots of problems. Clamps tend to slip on such a surface and constantly work loose. Trying to clamp a pair of planks to a stem is a prime example of such a situation. A workable solution is to attach a fixture next to your clamp in the direction of the slippage. Sometimes only the anvil side of the clamp will need this. The simplest fixture is a right-angle block with a step that gives purchase of the clamp and a longer leg that allows it to be attached to the plank. It should be positioned so that the clamping pressure is exerted over the joint and not in front of or behind it.

One type of fixture will suggest another. As your experience grows, so will your ingenuity. There are situations where no available clamp seems to work. You can substitute weight for clamps—bags of sand can even conform to odd shapes. You can use pressure from shores or external frameworks. You can use string, either wrapped or tightened by a Spanish windlass, or you can try a band clamp. You can use wedges and any combination of the above.

Clamping is a game that calls for flexibility, cunning, and perseverance, but it is the essence of boatbuilding, too—using what you have to get the job done and solving your own problems in your own way as they arise.

9. Preparing the Rough Plank

There is no single "hardest" job in building a boat—they all have their ups and downs. But planking has always called for skill and perseverance. Now, with taped-seam construction, the edge-to-edge fit of planks is no longer a strict requirement. Gaps of ¼ inch or even more are acceptable (in terms of the watertight integrity of the hull), so a lot of the burden is lifted from your shoulders. But planking is still an important job, and one that you will want to do right.

A good way to approach planking is to see it as a multiple-step process, with a higher degree of accuracy being required in each step. If this is your first boat, or if you are nervous about planking, you can follow each step in sequence, giving yourself an adequate margin for error for each one.

Plank fitting can be broken down into four steps:

1. Determining the rough plank shape and cutting it out slightly oversize.
2. Scarfing the plywood into rough planks.
3. Fitting one edge of the plank.
4. Fitting the other edge.

You can check your work at any stage and, if some margin for error has been left, you can correct any problems then and there.

Since the plank shapes are given directly in the drawings for the designs in this book, you may wonder why you can't just use them as they are. Indeed you can, with this proviso: Any deviation in your molds and setup from the ones in the drawings will produce different planks. Some of the errors can be insignificant, but sometimes a very small change in angle or location of a chine can cause a more significant difference, particularly at the ends of the boat where the most sweep in plank shapes occurs.

This gets us right into the heart of the matter—planks are flat boards, cut and made on flat benches, and yet they are wrapped around curved, beveled surfaces that make them take the oddest shapes.

The effect of flaring sides on a boat is to make her plank ends appear to shoot up higher than at the center; a straight-edged plank will look concave on its upper edge. Conversely, a plank which seems fairly straight when seen on a boat may actually be curved in some very unpredictable ways when laid out flat on the bench.

Convention dictates that planks on a boat generally appear somewhat straight, with a slight upward curve at the ends. They should run more or less parallel to the sheerline and to one another. Downsweep—"moose shoulders"—in the ends is considered unattractive. There is an overall look that we are trying to achieve in planking a hull, and we deviate from it at the risk of having our boat come out not looking quite right.

The process of making it look right is known as lining out the plank. It calls for patience, experience, a good eye, and a lot of battening off of the molds until you are satisfied with the way things look. If you were building from scratch, you would need to take this step before you could plank. The designs in this book give you a headstart by providing the plank shapes drawn out using a baseline and stations. Nevertheless, I recommend that rather than blindly drawing these curved shapes on your planking stock and cutting out what you assume will be a perfectly fitting plank, you cut out each plank a bit oversize at first, then determine its final shape with a batten while holding it in place against the molds. I'll cover the final fitting in more detail in Chapter 10. Right now let's return to the first two plank-fitting steps mentioned above. These need to be discussed in the same breath, because it's best to locate the scarf positions before cutting out each oversized blank, and it's best to cut out the blanks before gluing the scarfs.

Scarfs and Butts

There are two ways to join the ends of planks together—scarfs or butts.

Butt joints are definitely quick and dirty. You place the two pieces together end-to-end and back up the joint with a butt block, probably made from a similar thickness of material.

In the thin planking for the designs in this book, the butt is out of place. First, butts are prime targets for rot. Second, a butt joint, with its abrupt transition from single to double thickness, does not bend well and thus is a stress concentrator.

A scarf joint is far and away the superior method. Unfortunately, the thought of it frightens people off, although it is actually easy enough to make.

Figure 9–8 shows a simple slash scarf consisting of two overlapping bevels. The scarf is strong because it develops a lot of glued surface area in the joint. The pieces slide one by the other so the fit is forgiving. A bevel distributes the stress on the joint much more evenly than a butt does, and makes it a better joint for pieces that need to be bent or twisted. In fact, the only requirement is that the bevel be flat. Curved bevels— especially convex ones—don't glue up very well.

Placement of Scarfs

Before you can scarf up any plank stock, it is necessary to determine where the scarfs will fall on the boat. If possible, scarfs should lie in the forward and after thirds of the boat—in other words, in the ends rather than the middle of the hull. However, properly made epoxy scarfs are strong enough to go just about anywhere.

Figure 9-1. Ideal scarf placement. The scarfs should fall in the ends of the boat, with alternating runs of plank scarfed at opposite ends. Scarf lines should be approximately vertical, and scarfs in the same end should line up visually.

Accepted practice states that the scarfs in a boat should not lie one on top of another, all in a row, and for the old-style clenched scarfs this was quite true. If one row of planks is scarfed in the forward third of the boat, the next row is best scarfed in the aft third, and so on in alternating fashion.

You may only be able to purchase 8-foot lengths of 4 mm plywood. In the 11-foot canoe this means that you can scarf 8-foot and 4-foot lengths of ply to make 12-foot planks, and everything works out perfectly for staggering the scarfs as described.

With the 16-foot kayak you may be forced to place all the scarfs one over another in the middle of the boat, which seems to break every rule I just mentioned. But it is just what I did on the prototype of this boat, and although the traditionalist in me was offended, the boat seems none the weaker for it. I'm sure the fact that the already very strong scarfs are reinforced by the taping of the seams has a lot to do with this.

Strength aside, the layout and placement of the scarfs in your boat, especially in an open canoe, is an important aesthetic factor, so give it some thought. Keep the scarfs vertical and align the ones that are supposed to be in line so they don't look haphazardly strewn about the hull.

Positioning Rough Planks for Scarfing

In order to scarf up a rough plank (sometimes referred to as a blank) it is necessary to get the two component pieces overlapped properly and at the right angle to one another so that they very nearly describe the curve the finished plank will take.

There are two approaches to doing this. They are really variations on one another, the difference being in the rigorousness of the approach.

One way is to draw the grid from the plank shape drawing full size, to spot in the points, draw the plank outline, and lay the plywood over it. It is a slower, more exacting method but is safe and good for first-time plankers and anyone lacking confidence. The method is discussed in detail in Figures 9–2 through 9–4.

The second method is to lay pieces of plywood 2 feet wide (narrower if you wish) by 8 feet long across sawhorses or across a few planks that

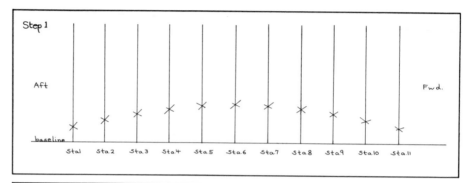

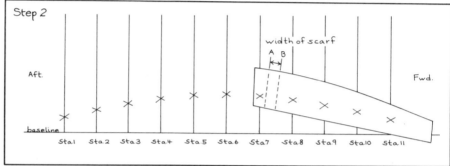

Figure 9-2. Positioning rough planks for scarfing, steps 1 and 2: (1) Draw a full-size grid with baseline and stations, longer than the longest plank. Space the stations according to the measured plank drawings. (Eleven stations are shown here for illustrative purposes, but our tack-and-tape boats have fewer stations to have to deal with.) To rough in a plank edge, measure points for each station as a height above the base. For absolute confidence in the process, you may wish to sweep a fair curve through these with a batten, and perhaps repeat the process with the other plank edge. (2) Working with the inner face of the plank uppermost, lay the forward portion of the rough blank on the grid so that the spotted points are comfortably covered by one edge of the blank. Draw line A approximately vertical (perpendicular to the baseline). Draw line B parallel to A and separated by the desired width of the scarf. (The lines are shown with a pronounced slope here; it's better that they be more nearly vertical.)

make up a crude bench (see Chapter 4 and Figure 10–2). Stretch a string for a baseline (or use a board or batten if you have one nearly straight and long enough), and cock the plywood pieces up at an angle that reproduces the angle of the planks in the drawing. Mark off the vertical stations specified in the plank shape drawing on your planking bench (if you have gone that route). If you mark them directly on the plywood instead, remember that angling or otherwise shifting the plywood will alter their positioning. Keep these at least approximately right, redrawing them when necessary. By measuring down to your baseline along these stations you can see if the point that defines the plank edge is on or off your plywood, and by how much. A little quick shuffling and you can

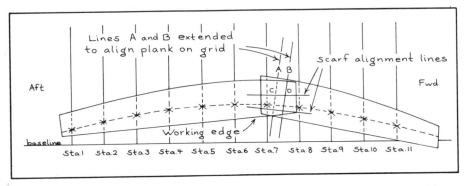

Figure 9-3. *Positioning rough planks for scarfing, step 3: Lay the after portion of the blank over the forward portion, making sure its working edge covers all the points. Be particularly careful of this in the area of the scarf. Transfer lines A and B to the after portion, labeling them as C and D respectively. This is easily done if the plank underneath is wider than the one on top. If it is not, extend lines A and B onto the drawing platform, or invent some other way to effect a transfer of the scarf lines. With a straightedge, draw one or two alignment marks across both planks. Now cut the after portion of the blank along line D, and the forward portion along line A. Bevel the mating surfaces of the scarf.*

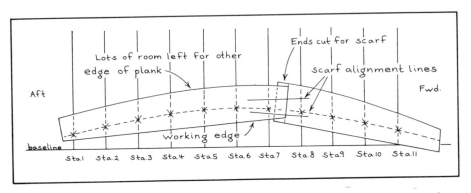

Figure 9-4. *With the bevels complete, realign the plank portions with reference to the alignment marks. The plank can be glued on the grid to ensure proper alignment. Use waxed paper under the scarf to avoid gluing the plank to the grid. The finished blank becomes a pattern for its mirror-image counterpart on the opposite side of the boat. Use the outside face of the existing blank to give the shape for the inside face of its opposite.*

have the pieces aligned well enough to create an oversized blank that can be cut down later. In fact, you can be pretty accurate if you try.

Place the forward and aft sections of the plank so that the overlap for the scarf falls in the right place, and mark the cut line for the scarf so that it will be more or less vertical on the boat. (An alignment that seems vertical on the planking bench turns out to be so in the finished boat as well.) Use a straightedge to make one or two alignment marks, and you're in business.

If this seems a little slapdash, it is. But it is fast and efficient, and not all that scary after you've made a few planks. Read the section on margins for error to be comforted even more. With the right margin for error you can get this blank right and use it as a pattern to make the next with almost no need for "a little extra," especially if you don't mind spending the extra time to make the actual plank from it first, and then use that as a pattern.

Margins for Error

When cutting a plank you are confident of, an inch of margin for each edge can be a princely amount. But it's wise to leave 2 to 4 inches if there is some question. Then too, the same margin may not be needed all along the plank. Sometimes only ½ inch may be enough in the center of the sweep, while 4 inches may be needed in the ends.

Apart from how easily the molds faired, and how faithful you were to the original dimensions, there are several points to help guide you.

Do not be afraid to generate a little scrap. I know that planking material can be expensive, but some scrap is inevitable. If the plans call for two sheets of plywood for planking, saving a quarter sheet may be a self-imposed handicap and only result in some unused rippings gathering dust and taking up space. You will have spent two sheets worth of money anyway, and unless another boat is looming up in your life soon, the effort could be a wasted one.

Since you can use a given plank on one side of the boat as the reverse pattern for its mate on the other, it follows that you need only give a generous margin to one. Why not use the margin for both in the one, and be sure of getting it right? When all else is said and done, there is nothing as wasteful as making the same plank twice.

Cutting a Scarf

The first step is to lay out the joint. The rule of thumb is that the length of a scarf should be 12 times the thickness of the material joined. Convention and common sense further require that the outside bevel taper off to the stern rather than forward, so that any protruding edge will be less likely to catch debris in the water.

This means that you will cut the forward scarf on one face of the stock, and the after scarf on the opposite face. Drawing a simple sketch and labeling the two planks will help keep you from getting confused during the layout.

It may be helpful to draw layout lines on the edge of the plank as well, to mark the beginning and end of each cut, although this can be impractical on very thin plywood. Better indicators are the different layers of veneer, which will show up as bands as you cut. They can be a real

Figure 9-5. A partially cut scarf showing a limit line (for the width of the scarf) penciled in. Note scalloped surface from scrub plane.

Figure 9-6. Checking the finished scarf for flatness. Scallops have been removed with a jointer plane working across the scarf.

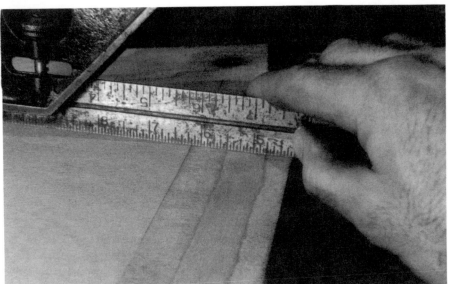

aid in keeping your cut even—too deep a cut on one side will make the bands appear wider there. By keeping the bands even, you keep the cut even as well.

The real key to good scarfing is rapid stock removal. I like to waste (remove) 95 percent of the excess wood immediately and roughly. I use either a fishtail gouge or a scrub plane with a radiused profile cutter. On heavier stock (but not on plywood) I have used a circular saw and even a hatchet.

Figure 9-7. A jointer plane and a scrub plane, both useful for scarfing.

If you use a regular plane with a flat cutter, the work will be slow and frustrating, and you'll very likely end up with a bevel at the wrong angle. The rough tools leave a scalloped surface that is easily brought to the right pitch and bevel and then finished.

I usually go right from the rough tools to a *sharp* No. 7 jointer plane. Generally I plane across the joint rather than with the long grain. If you have done your removal well, the joiner work can really be only a few strokes. You know you're done when the bumps are removed and the cutter is slicing off the width of the scarf and not just the tops of the individual scallops.

I work on a long, flat bench with the edge of the bevel right at the end of the bench. This gives it support no matter how thin the tip of the bevel, while still allowing clearance for the plane body.

You do not want a perfect feather edge at the bevel. There is too much danger that you will tear the grain in the process, and it seems to glue better if the edge is not quite feathered. One-sixteenth of an inch is too much; one thirty-second of an inch or less is about right. You can get away with one that's a bit thick, but it won't look quite as good.

For convenience, I usually scarf my stock longer than the finished plank will be. I size my planks after the glue has set. That way, if something has slipped a little, all is not lost.

Gluing the Scarf

I find it easiest to lay the pieces out on my assembly table and to pile weights—lead ballast, water buckets, or whatever—on top of a single pressure pad made of a scrap of plywood just slightly bigger than the scarf. Make sure the pressure of the weights is evenly distributed. I use waxed paper over the table and under the pressure pad so that nothing gets glued that shouldn't.

The two glued pieces will slide around on one another with frightening ease, so careful alignment and checking is in order. When all is right, I apply a pair of clamps on either side of the joint to prevent movement. I usually clamp the bottom piece to the table (waxed paper under it) before putting the top one down on it so that only one piece can move during alignment. It never hurts to reduce the number of variables!

Figure 9-8. Recommended scarf layout and glue-up. The pressure pad on top of the glue-up should ideally be the same material as the plank and slightly longer and wider than the scarf. Its ends should be clamped to prevent movement of the pieces and to create a light pressure on the joint. Place waxed paper under the pad and under the plank.

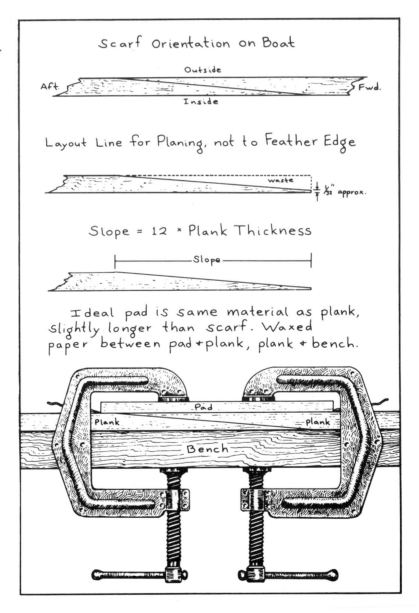

Scarf Orientation on Boat

Outside

Aft

Inside

Fwd.

Layout Line for Planing, not to Feather Edge

waste

$\frac{1}{32}''$ approx.

Slope = 12 × Plank Thickness

Slope

Ideal pad is same material as plank, slightly longer than scarf. Waxed paper between pad + plank, plank + bench.

Pad

Plank

plank

Bench

Since plywood end-grain is absorbent, you may need to put the glue on several times, say at 15-minute intervals, to saturate the grain. This depends on the ambient temperature and the viscosity of the glue. After a few minutes, the wood will turn dull where the glue has been soaked up, and stay shiny where it hasn't. When both scarf surfaces remain shiny, they are ready to be joined. If you aren't careful about this, the end-grain will draw the glue away from the joint, and there will be no strength when it dries. The result is a "starved" joint.

Overapplication may be safe, but it is messy, especially with epoxy. You want just a little squeeze-out when you put the pressure on. Once you learn to put on the right amount, your clean-up and finishing will be much easier.

You do not need excessive pressure to glue epoxies—bringing the pieces together with a light, positive pressure should be sufficient. Too much squeeze will lead to starved joints.

When they are dry, clean the scarfs with a scraper, a sharp plane, and a belt sander. Try to handle the planks so as not to put undue stress on the joint. It's a good idea to carry them edge up, as opposed to flat. However, a little judicious testing off the boat is all to the good. If it's going to fail, now is a good time to find out. I always test my joints, and the rippings from oversized plank blanks are ideal for this.

10. Fitting and Joining Planks

Fitting the Edge

Once the blank has been scarfed and glued, the actual fitting can take place. Lay the blank on a convenient bench, table, or floor. Snap or otherwise set up a baseline and draw the correctly spaced station lines perpendicular to it, as in the drawings. This is for the final fit, so accuracy is required.

Set the blank down on this grid in the correct position (in relation to scarf placement), and pencil in the station lines where they cross the plank. Now measure up the station lines the offset distance, and mark the points of the curve. (If the offset distance turns out to be inconve-

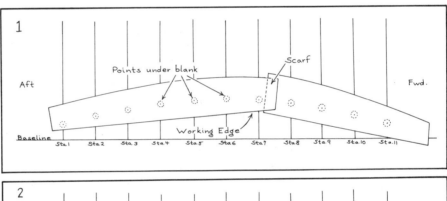

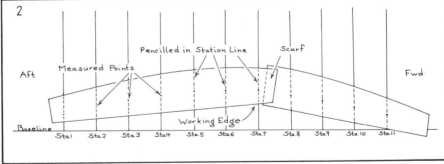

Figure 10-1. Drawing a finished plank shape onto a rough blank. The procedure is much like that illustrated in Figures 9-2 through 9-4, but there the objective was to ensure that the scarfed blank would be large enough and correctly shaped to permit cutting the finished plank from it. Here the objective is to get the finished plank. Once again a grid is established, plank-edge offsets are spotted in, and the blank is laid over these points, as shown in (1). But this time the next step is to clamp or tack the blank in its correct position, extend the station lines over the upper surface of the blank, and transfer the plank offsets onto this surface (2). Then fair in the plank-edge curve with a batten and pencil. Cut just outside this line, then plane down to the line, testing the edge fit against a batten over the molds (Figure 10-3) as you do so.

nient, you can add a fixed number to each offset and still get the same curve in the location you want.)

This step is exactly the process that you used to establish the rough curve, only more accurate. Spot in the other edge of the plank as well at this time if you wish.

Position the outer edge of the curve as close to the edge of the plywood blank as you can. This will leave the maximum amount of margin to work with. Cut to this line, leaving the pencil marks as a reference.

You may cut this with a bandsaw, if you have one, or a saber saw. Even a small circular saw blade, set only a little deeper than the material to be cut, can make a pretty decent curve without binding. By small I mean around 4½ inches, but even a 6-inch blade isn't too bad. Use a plywood blade, or one with a lot of teeth, or the splintering will be excessive.

If you use a saber saw, remember that the plank stock will need to be held tightly in place where the blade wants to pull it up. In getting a good cut, it's essential to keep the work from vibrating.

I cut as close to the line as I dare, or as my particular saw will allow. A splinter-prone tool will require more clearance. Let discretion be the better part of valor here. Don't go inside the pencil marks or otherwise lose them; they are the only reference you have.

After cutting, I use a sharp scrub plane with a fairly generous set to come right down to the line, hitting the high spots first, so that when I'm done I have an even fraction of waste all along the line. Then I plane just to the line with a sharp smooth plane so that only the pencil mark shows. I gradually work the entire line down, rather than trying to make one section perfect at a time. When I'm really close I try to make the last few cuts long, overlapping ones that will smooth out any local variations that exist.

I like to leave the pencil line so I know what I'm working to. But it also helps to eyeball the edge of the plank itself. Turn the plank over if the pencil line distracts your eye. What you want, in the end, is a continuous, fair line.

When you want to check the fit on this edge alone, clamp the plank in place (without cutting the other line). Use the station lines on the plank to align it on the molds. The edge should fit nicely against a fair batten tacked to the mold edges "around the corner" of the chine, as in Figure 10–3. If there is a problem, use dividers set to the largest difference to mark off the correction.

Remember that the curve of the plank is irregular, and shifting the plank forward or aft of where it is meant to go will compromise the fit. I pencil in two arrowheads that meet, one on the plank I'm fitting, and one on the boat or previous plank. This ensures accurate, repeatable registration of the plank in the same place every time. If you do not observe this type of precaution, you will find all kinds of puzzling and frustrating errors creeping into your work.

Figure 10-2. *A simple planking bench consisting of a 12-foot 2 × 12 on sawhorses is useful when measuring, cutting, and planing planks. A lead block (good for holding the plank while sighting an edge—use several), a scrub plane, and a smooth plane (for the final planing to a fair edge) are shown. The plank is worked on the flat, with its edge projecting just past the bench. Curved planks can be worked a section at a time by repositioning them on the bench as needed. Holding the plank down with one hand while you plane with the other is usually all the clamping you need.*

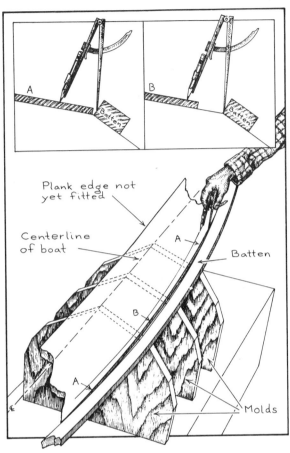

Figure 10-3. *Fitting the first edge of a plank. A batten is tacked over the molds, along the chine, as shown, and the plank is placed in position. In this instance the plank fits well at points A; the widest gap is at B. The pencil compass or dividers are adjusted to span the gap, and a line is drawn at that setting along the plank edge. Take care that the dividers remain parallel to the mold edges as the line is scribed. Plane the plank edge down to this line, and it should fit closely.*

After you've gotten the first edge, the second one is easy. Either measure off the correct distance on the station lines (taken from the offset table) or step off the actual distance on the molds with dividers and transfer it to the plank station lines. Of course, if you've changed the plank shapes very much, the latter method is better.

At this point you have a plank that fits where you want it, except that it is a little longer than it will be eventually. If you're building with a false stem, trim the plank to the correct length with a coping saw; if you're incorporating a real stem you can glue the plank end to the stem

Figure 10-4. Fitting a plank. Once you have the first edge of the plank fitted as in Figure 10-3, you can step off the plank width on the molds with dividers (1), and transfer these widths to the plank to establish its other edge (3). It's not a bad idea, since you'll be using this plank as a pattern for its opposite counterpart, to be sure the chine offset on the other side of each mold is the same, or nearly so, as on the first side (2).

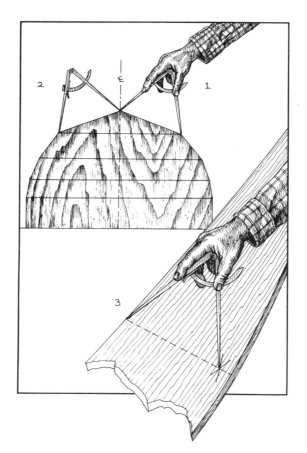

Figure 10-5. Marking planks as an aid to fitting them. The garboard is in place and the next plank down is being fitted. Planks are labeled as to which side of the boat they go on, which end is which, and whether the face showing is the inner or outer face. The station marks provide rough positioning, but the V's give final alignment accuracy whenever a plank is removed for a bit of additional planing, then repositioned. Here permanent stems and keel are shown, but these are optional. The plank ends are shown trimmed for clarity, although in practice you need not do this until you fit the mating plank on the opposite side.

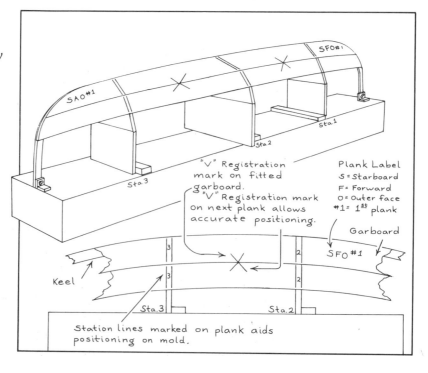

before trimming it, but in any event the plank end must be trimmed before the mating plank on the opposite side of the boat can be laid into position.

If you plan to use a plank as a pattern for its counterpart, do so before you fasten it to the molds. For fastening you will need a temporary means of holding the plank in place; using small, roundheaded woodworking screws (⅝- or ¾-inch) driven through buttons provides good positive holding, with the added bonus that the buttons (small square or rectangular pieces of plank scrap) can be located in the center of the plank and out of the way of the taping process. This is the best way to go when you are satisfied with the fit of the plank.

Continue these steps for each plank pair, from garboard to sheer, until all the planks are on the molds.

Joining the Planks

The final step in the planking process is to join the planks edge to edge using epoxy resin and fiberglass tape. You can use the stitch and glue method, or elect just to tape the seams.

In the stitch and glue approach, you drill a series of small holes in the plank edges and sew the boards together with light-gauge copper wire. This may sound outlandish, but it's a time-honored technique dating back to the Stone Age.

This method probably involves more work because the wiring is an extra step, since you need to tape the seams anyway. Also, the wire can show up as bumps or irregularities under the tape. Countersinking can help eliminate this, but is more work and not always totally successful.

Is there an advantage to stitch and glue? One advantage is that you need either no molds, or very few molds, since the wire can hold everything together until you tape. You can set up a single mold amidships, take your plank shapes from the drawings in the book, and sew up a boat.

With widely spaced molds such as we have here, and flexible 4 mm planking, there needs to be some edge-to-edge fastening of the planks to pull everything into the same plane and to eliminate bouncing of the planks while you are taping. At a minimum you will probably need to do some wire tying about halfway between molds, more if there is still too much flex or if the edges are curling due to any twist in the planks. This twist is most pronounced at the ends, and you may need to do more tying there. On these boats I found that I did several lacings between the stem (or stern) and the first mold.

What we are trying to do is to create a skin for the boat that is strong and watertight both inside and out. The first step is to cover the seams outside, smoothing and filling them as necessary. If the plank edges make a sharp angle or corner where they meet, you should round them off with a plane or sandpaper to make an easy radius. Fiberglass tape doesn't

Figure 10-6. A pair of garboards in place on the canoe. Note the spring clamps to hold them to the stem pattern and/or each other, and the use of a batten against which to fit the plank (not necessary with measured drawings, but recommended nevertheless). A screw and button can be seen holding the planks to the mold.

Figure 10-7. Kayak bow with port garboard in place. Note buttons to hold plank in place (see Figure 10-9).

Figure 10-8. Kayak bow, both garboards in place, false stem removed preparatory to taping the garboard seam. Spring clamps hold ends of planks together before planks are drilled for wire ties.

Figure 10-9. Buttons made from planking scrap hold the planks on the molds. They are easy to use and conveniently clear of the seams, but are too far from the plank edges to hold down a curled edge or stabilize a bouncy edge joint. For these problems you will need to use wire ties.

EASY OR HARD

As with any job, knowing the right procedure can make all the difference between what is a difficult task and an impossible one. Several examples, with far-reaching applications, will clarify what I mean.

On symmetrical hulls there is no advantage to beginning a rail or a plank at either the bow or stern, or even the middle, when bending it on. But with asymmetrical hulls there can be a marked difference.

Many kayaks have their greatest beam aft of amidships, and thus the curvature of the sheer into the stern is much sharper than the longer, easier taper at the bow. Here there is a decided advantage to beginning at the stern and using the length of the workpiece to lever in the proper bend. Saving the hardest part of the curve for last makes the job much more difficult.

In addition to the lever advantage that a longer piece of rail gives you, you may hold the plank or rail out from the hull at whatever angle is necessary in order to get the first foot or so to lie snugly against the hull. Once the clamps or screws are tightened down on this part and the piece is firmly in place, you can slowly work the rest of it into the proper plane. On a kayak rail that is being held with light screws of severely limited pulling power and no good way to use clamps (because the deck is on), this may be the only way that you can get a reluctant bend tightly into place.

The idea of "easy" and "hard" ends is a valuable technique that applies to planking, decks, and almost any bent or fitted piece. A little foresight can make the difference between a struggle and a straightforward installation. Situations that will respond to this treatment usually advertise their presence by a rapidly changing bevel or radius of curvature.

The design of joints can also make your job easier or harder. In this area, following the older rules of thumb or accepted practice is usually a safe guide to the right way to proceed. Boatbuilders have pretty much figured out how to do things through the passing centuries.

A good example is the connection between the inwale and the breasthook. This is usually accomplished by means of a long, overlapping bevel. You may wonder why this is done, reasoning that a simple square cut would be easier than two bevels.

The reason is twofold. First, the bevels give much more glue area and are therefore much stronger. But they also offer an ease of fit that should not be underestimated.

It should be noted that on the square cut the angle will seldom be truly square, so some form of bevel will be needed no matter what. And this joint involves gluing end-grain to end-grain, which is mechanically very weak. Finally, and quite important to us, the joint offers very little margin for error. It either fits or it doesn't. If the inwale is too short it simply won't fit. There is no gray area wherein the two pieces slide by one another. With overlapping bevels, if the piece is a little too short or too long the joint can still be closed.

In fact this style of joint might be called a "closing" joint, because the tendency is for the workpiece (the inwale in this case) to close the joint as it is fitted into place. The natural bend of the inwale will tend to push it into position, and all you need to do is create the proper conditions for it to do so.

Finally, the actual process of putting the pieces together is much simpler with the bevels. Trying to clamp the square-cut joint is an exercise in impossibility or sheer frustration.

MARKING

A few small pencil marks can often spell the difference between ease and difficulty in performing certain tasks.

The long curved edge of a plank should be smooth, with easy transitions and a good fair line. As mentioned earlier, you need a gauge mark so that you can accurately reposition the plank each time you take it off the boat to work it.

It is easy to lose your place on a long curve so I use pencil marks here also, as well as using the irregularities of the grain as landmarks. The curve is best sighted with your eye right down on the line (which is not a good position to plane from).

I usually use a single vertical line to mark the beginning or end of a given section or plank. This segment could be either hollow, in which case I'll want to stay out of it, or it could be a high spot that I'll want to take down. I use a squiggly line between end marks to mean I should plane that whole section or stay out of it, depending on the particular case. For smaller spots, I use X's to show where I need to plane, and O's to show the parts to leave alone. Use any system that works for you.

In joints where I can't actually see what is taking place, I use two other techniques. One is to use the regular powdered chalk for chalk lines to find the high spots. I put the chalk on the piece I'm fitting to. When the workpiece comes in contact with it, the chalk will transfer to the high spots.

I also use a regular mechanic's feeler gauge. I slip the metal leaf into the joint and try to slide it around. It won't be able to move at all in the high spots, and will slide easily where the open areas are. A good, snug slide means a good fit. The feeler gauge will let you pick the tolerance you want right down to the nearest thousandth of an inch.

Don't underestimate your sense of touch, either. Fingertips can detect little bumps, high spots, and rounded bevels—to mention only a few irregularities—and they can do the job quite well.

The important part is to correlate this information (where the high spots or hollows are) to the actual work. The process of making a fit is really just selectively removing material, and you need to know where to do the removing. Pencil marks can be invaluable here. Not only can they show you where to cut, but if you put them on the offending spot itself, they can tell you if you are in fact cutting there. For example, if I have a rounded bevel I'll pencil in the top of the round. Seeing the pencil marks disappear means that I am planing at the correct angle. If I'm making shavings but the pencil marks remain, it means that I'm holding the plane at the wrong angle and I'd better find the right one.

like sharp corners—it won't make the bend, and voids or bubbles will form, leading to poor adherence.

Only after the outside seams are completely taped and the resin cured will you lift the boat from the molds, turn it over, and then, with the molds no longer interfering, finish the inside seams. These present the same problems but need a different solution. Before you can tape, you need to mix up some glue and filler to make a paste, and "fillet" the seam to make a nice, rounded radius rather than leaving a sharp angle.

Figure 10-10. A bouncy edge makes it very hard (maybe impossible) to stipple on resin while taping the seams because the movement of the plank makes it want to pull away from the tape. Tying the edges together at intervals is the answer. One or two ties between molds is probably inevitable, and you may need more in the ends, where the planks twist toward the vertical. How many depends on how well the plank fits the mold and how far apart the molds are, how stiff the planking material is, etc. Shown here is a detail of a wire tie lacing a pair of plank edges together. The wire fits in a groove made with a rasp, allowing it to lie flat under the tape. I use very light copper wire, about 26 gauge, usually doubled through the holes, pulled tight with a plier in each hand, and twisted together. Some tightening by twisting is possible before the wire breaks, but use a light touch or heavier wire if breaking is a problem.

Figure 10-11. Detail of lacing ends together at stem. Opposing planks are sewn together and then laced to the pair above and below.

Figure 10-12. After buttoning, wire-tying, or otherwise fastening the plank in a good edge-to-edge orientation, you are ready to tape the outside seams. It is essential that no plank edge be higher or lower than the one it mates to; they need to be in the same plane or you won't get maximum wood-to-wood contact for the tape. If the planks meet at a pronounced angle so a hard edge is formed, you will need to radius the edge before taping.

The first step is to brush on resin to wet out the plywood and to form a bed for the tape. Two-inch tape is a good width for most cases, but 3-inch gives extra coverage, which is good, too. I think the 2-inch is a little neater. With only an inch of overlap on each side, it's important to keep the tape well centered over the seam. After laying in the tape, the next step is to dab or stipple on more resin to wet it out. Dab with a brush using an up and down motion; do not brush normally or you will probably move, wrinkle, or otherwise foul up the tape. Give the tape time to wet out, as evidenced by a darkening of color. Resist the temptation to apply too much resin; the tape tends to float on it, which inhibits its bond to the wood and will make the boat too heavy.

The dark areas show where the tape has been successfully wetted out. Lighter areas indicate dry spots, bubbles, or areas where the tape isn't in contact with the wood. It's okay not to start the tape all the way up in the bow; your later stem work can make up for it.

Note how the stem taping is being put on in small athwartship patches to accommodate the stem's curve. A single piece of tape down the stem would not follow the curve without problems such as lifted edges or air bubbles, since the tape would need to curve in too many directions at once. Several layers of staggered patches will do the job nicely. These first three patches are meant to provide a foundation and to hold the plank ends together.

You can use your gloved finger or employ a thin strip of wood with the right radius worked into one end. Sometimes a tongue depressor works. Overfill the seam and pull your finger or filleting stick along to take off the excess. Keep it as smooth as you can, because any bumps or snags will make voids when you tape.

Laying the tape into a freshly made fillet, before it has set up, is a very good way to avoid bumps or snags, since the tape will flatten them out and conform to the irregularities of the surface. It's a good way to save time, too. Just remember to brush a coat of resin on top of the fillet before you tape, just as you would do for bare wood.

If you aren't using a keel and stems, you will need to fillet and tape these seams as well. It may take more glue and filler than you suspect. The stem area is vertical, without a lot of clearance, making work there fussy and frustrating. The same prohibition against rough spots holds here, too. Any voids, which will weaken the holding power of the tape, can be especially disastrous in the stem.

A single layer of tape won't be strong enough to do the job adequately. I use two layers of tape over the entire boat, inside and out, with three layers in stress spots.

Before you start, it's good to mark out the area that you want to tape. Use pencil dividers or a wooden block cut to the right dimension and make a continuous line to get an edge mark. This gives you a guideline for applying the resin, but more important, it helps you apply the tape to get good, even coverage and a straight run.

Figure 10-13. A close-up view of the seam shown in Figure 10-12—now nicely wet out. See the wire tie under it, in the groove that lets it lie below the plank surface. The 2-inch tape is pretty well divided over the seam.

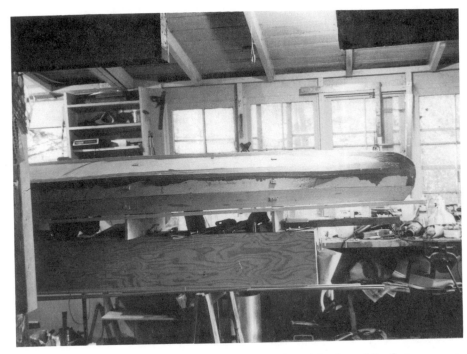

Figure 10-14. The same seam later on. Both the garboard (keel) and the first seam are taped. More stem taping has been added. The sheer plank is in place as well. The edge-to-edge fit of the planks is pretty tight, which is not essential structurally or aesthetically (it all gets buried under the tape), but certainly makes applying the first layer of tape easier, and provides a certain satisfaction as well.

Figure 10-15. A look at the next seam to be taped will help us summarize the process. First the resin is brushed on . . .

Figure 10-16. . . . then the precut length of tape is laid into position. Overlapping folds make the tape up into an easily handled bundle. Note the rubber gloves. Your hands are the best tools for this job, and the gloves are to protect them. On a vertical surface like this one, unfold only a short length of tape at a time and make sure it is well stuck before you go on—or gravity will make your job very difficult indeed. . . .

Figure 10-17. . . . Finally, once the tape is on, use your gloved fingers to smooth it, straighten it, and work out any wrinkles. Pulling on the tape from opposite sides of a wrinkle is a good way to flatten it out. Working from the center of the tape out to the edges is good technique, especially important with bigger pieces of cloth.

When you're using cloth to sheath the garboards or deck, it should be precut to roughly fit the necessary area. Exact fits are hard to achieve with cloth, due to its stretchable nature and the way it slides about. You'll need to use oversized pieces and trim them to exact size later.

Wear a pair of disposable gloves when you apply resin to the raw wood. Resin can be applied with a brush, but it's easier and quicker to squeegee it on with a flexible plastic card, at least for big, fairly flat surfaces. You can use a thin piece of wood, metal, or Formica for the same purpose. Pour the resin on, and spread it around with the card. The edge can be notched like the edge of a tile cement trowel. It's easy to scrape off too much resin with an un-notched card, leaving the plywood surface too dry to make a good bond.

The resin should be thin enough to spread easily and to wet out the cloth. Use a resin formulated for laminating or sheathing rather than a thick, viscous epoxy glue formulated for its gap-filling qualities. Too thick a resin is a disaster in every aspect, with failure just about guaranteed.

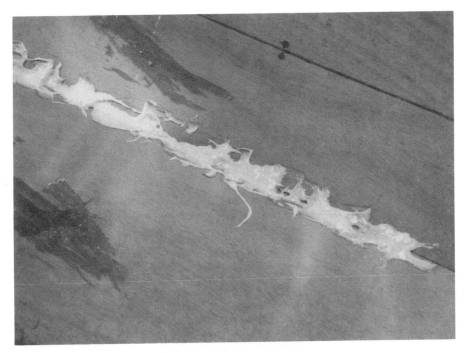

Figure 10-18. Taping an inside seam. The joint is the keel, where the kayak garboards meet. The angle is too steep for the tape to lie well in the apex, so thickened resin is being laid into the joint preparatory to making a fillet. A wire tie can be seen at the top. Wire ties can get in the way on inside seams, since tightening them tends to pull them up above the plank surface, especially if the planks meet at an angle. Since the outside seams are already taped, you could cut the offending wire with diagonal cutters and pull the strands out with pliers. If the wire gets in the way of making a nice continuous fillet this is always a good idea.

Figure 10-19. The same seam. A rounded scrap of plywood is used to trowel the resin into a nicely rounded fillet.

Figure 10-20. Front view of the same process. There is too much resin used and the blob will leak around the trowel, but this excess can be easily removed with a putty knife before it sets. If you get the right amount, the slight amount of extra glue keeps feeding the trowel and you can make one long fillet with no spillover or mess.

The next step is to brush straight resin on the fillet and to lay in the tape as for an outside seam. Not waiting for the fillet to set speeds up the job and makes it very easy to lay the tape, since the one can accommodate the other while they are both flexible. A light touch in laying the tape and brushing on subsequent resin is good to cultivate or you can distort the fillet. Finding the right consistency of resin and filler will help, too.

Putting on too much resin is a common mistake, especially as a cure-all for bubbles and folds. Not only is it expensive, but it will make your boat heavier than it needs to be. It also makes the job more difficult, because the cloth wants to float on top of the resin rather than adhere to the plywood. Try to use just enough resin to saturate the cloth.

Once the resin is spread, you—and a helper if at all possible—can stretch the cloth out above the entire area and lower it down into the resin. The cloth will tend to stick where it touches the resin, so position it carefully. If you're working alone, you can use pieces of waxed paper or clean sticks to keep the cloth from getting prematurely embedded in the resin. Later you can carefully work them out from under the cloth.

Try to remove any large wrinkles or bubbles before pressing the cloth down. You can usually stretch or pull these out. Sometimes simultaneous pulling in opposite directions does the trick.

Pat the cloth down into the resin so that it sticks. The resin will start to bleed through the cloth where it is adhering. Be careful not to move the cloth from side to side or to pull it. Just try to press it straight down. The same applies to tape, although tape is easier to work because it is narrower.

When this is done, use a disposable bristle brush to stipple more resin into the cloth, to wet it out. The correct brush action is an up-and-down dabbing—conventional back-and-forth brushing will drag the cloth and make folds or bubbles.

On any piece of cloth or tape, work from the center out, pushing trapped air toward the edge where it can dissipate. Resin is too thick for

Figure 10-21. The completed inside seam, with tape laid into a resined fillet and wetted out. Except for filleting, the operation is the same as for an outside seam.

Figure 10-22. The best place for your gloves is right on the mold, clipped into a pair of wooden clothes pins, which keeps them handy and lets them dry inside and out after use.

Figure 10-23. Glass tape before grinding, showing rough edges, "snags," etc.

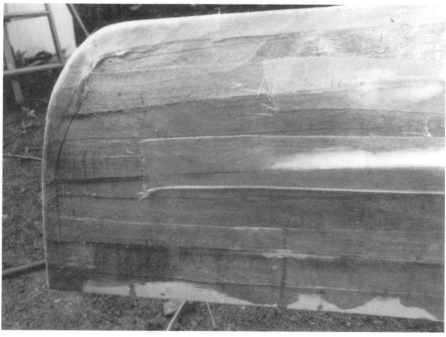

the air to bubble through, and if there is air under the cloth it will appear milky. A uniform darkening of the cloth as it saturates will indicate your progress. Cloth that lies against the wood will be dark and transparent. Give the resin time to penetrate the cloth, since the color change is not instantaneous.

Excess cloth must be trimmed away at the proper time. If you try to trim before the resin has set up, you will almost invariably move the cloth, and probably wrinkle it to boot. On the other hand, resin and cloth that has set up is quite hard. It can nick steel tools and dull any edge. If you wait until the resin is semicured, it will be sticky enough to hold the cloth, but simple to cut. A utility knife with a sharp blade is all you need.

Only in special circumstances is it necessary to let the resin cure completely before you apply the next layer of cloth or tape. In the bow, for example, where the planks are particularly springy and will probably need to be stitched before taping, allowing a complete cure between layers makes sense logistically.

Once the resin of the final layer has cured it is usual to apply one or two more coats to fill in the weave of the cloth and to make a smoother surface. Finally, grind the surface as described in the accompanying photographs.

The entire job of sheathing or taping will go much more easily if you have gravity working for you to hold the cloth against the wood. With small craft, it makes sense to tip or turn the hull to achieve that condi-

Figure 10-24. After grinding: All edges feathered off, snags and rough spots ground down. At the stem you may want to put on one layer, let it set up, and then grind it smooth, touching up the radiusing before the next layer. This lets one layer improve the next instead of making it harder to do right. As the tape goes on, it thickens the stem and the radius gets easier to wrap the tape around, so that the last layers can be much easier than the first. Grinding between layers can help that, too.

Figure 10-25. Drill and abrasive disk (Number 24 grit) used in grinding. Wear eye protection and a respirator. The disk cuts best if it is moved somewhat diagonally across the work as it rotates. Let the tool work freely; bearing down too hard will just load up the disk.

tion. If you can't arrange that, use masking tape to hold the cloth in position.

Really curved or compound surfaces will be easier to do in several pieces. Small patches put on in a staggered buildup will do a better, smoother job than if you try too large a piece. When they set up they are the same as if they had been applied at once, so give yourself a break. Where the seams overlap, you can sand them smooth. In the canoe the curve of the forefoot is just such an area, and will benefit from this approach.

11. Breasthooks and Rails

I in a glued and taped boat, the rails and breasthooks form the major structural features apart from the planking, strengthening and giving shape to what is essentially a flexible structure.

They also play an important role in the appearance of the boat, since they constitute the major feature of internal finish in an open canoe. Components that are poorly proportioned—especially if they are heavy looking—destroy the otherwise light and delicate feeling these boats can project.

Breasthooks

Perhaps the most vulnerable part of a boat is where the planking comes together at the stem, especially at the sheer. Not only is this area subject to strong wracking and twisting forces, but it is exposed to sudden shock loads in the form of collisions and bumps. In addition to the twisting forces applied, there is a certain amount of transverse force trying to spread the planks apart. Early on in the history of the boat a need for reinforcement was seen, and the breasthook was the result.

The breasthook is a triangular piece of blocking that fits into the shape formed by the converging sheerplanks and stem (see Figure 11–13). Its function is to tie these elements together, and it usually provides a means of attachment for the inwale as well.

For all these reasons, breasthooks should be solidly attached. Although they are bolted in larger craft, a glue joint is more than adequate for our purpose. The breasthook legs parallel to the planking need to be long enough to give some holding area, ensuring that the resultant structure is an effective brace.

In a solo canoe, a breasthook with a length of around 4½ inches is fine. A bigger canoe may require a few more inches, while a decked boat can get away with less, or perhaps even let the inwale ends substitute for a breasthook.

Since wood is strongest along the grain, breasthooks should be made in such a way that the grain runs parallel to the planking. This means using natural crooks or gluing up two pieces of stock so that the grains are convergent.

Getting my measurements from the boat, I plan the breasthook blank so it will be a little oversized. A pattern is useful in laying out the pieces, not only to get them symmetrical, but as an aid in orienting the grain, which will seem to be lying at an angle to the orientation your eye might naturally choose. A transparent pattern is good here, but I get fine results by using a plywood pattern with a penciled arrow on it that rep-

Figure 11-1. A breasthook for the open canoe. It should be glued from two pieces so that the grain in each parallels the outside edge. A transverse crown is desirable. Only one rail is shown here, for clarity.

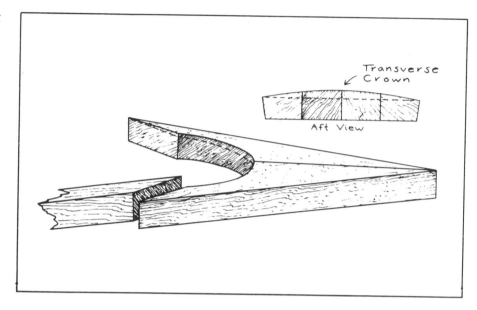

Figure 11-2. Breasthook blanks ready to glue. The grain direction, parallel to the planking, is laid out with the help of a pattern. These blanks are oversized, being wider than the finished pieces.

resents the necessary run of grain. Just align the arrow with the grain in the stock, and trace.

Joining the two halves of the breasthook should be done with care, because you need a strong joint with no gaps or weakness. I find a long hand jointer plane to be best. Often fixing the plane in a bench vise, sole up, and moving the workpiece across it is the best method. The pieces are too small to be safely or successfully worked on a power jointer, but you could joint a longer piece of stock first, and cut the breasthook parts out of that, saving the good edge for where they join. To check the joint,

Figure 11-3. Running a breasthook blank over a jointer plane held in a vise. This is a good way to work small pieces that would otherwise be awkward. To check for a good fit, butt the breasthook pieces in front of a strong light source and see if light bleeds through. Get the best fit you can here; this piece needs to be strong. It can be reinforced with a screw as discussed in the text, but it needs to be carefully fitted and ready to glue before you fasten it. Since the blanks are oversized, you have enough material to get a good fit, even if you take a lot off.

I butt the pieces together in front of a good light source and look for light bleeding through any gaps.

The triangular shape is a little tricky to clamp. I set one piece in a vise, positioned so that the top edge of the piece that sits on top of it will be horizontal. I use some spring clamps or small C-clamps right on the joint, to keep edge alignment and to stop any slippage. Then I rest a 3- or 4-pound block of lead on the uppermost edge of the top piece to press everything together, letting gravity do the work.

I don't attempt to cut the breasthook blank to actual size until the glue is dry. This is easier than worrying about exact alignment during the glue-up. To fit the breasthook, I first doublecheck that the sheer planks are planed right down to their lines, their top edges are at equal height, and the curves are fair and true. Then I place a straightedge across them where the breasthook will be fitted and measure the angle between the straightedge and the insides of the sheer planks. This gives the side bevel needed on the "legs" of the breasthook.

Usually this bevel will change slightly from one end of the breasthook to the other, generally on the order of a few shavings, but possibly

Figure 11-4. Gluing up breasthook blanks. Note small C-clamps to stop top piece from sliding out of alignment and to force edge alignment, and the use of lead weights to create clamping pressure. Another pair of C-clamps at the end of the joint would be okay. The whole assembly is held in a bench vise so that the glue joint is horizontal, helping reduce its tendency to creep.

Figure 11-5. A rough blank—glued up. It is still oversized at this point, but now ready to be marked and cut to fit. Use the glue joint as a centerline, and measure outward from there the widths you need at the forward and aft ends. Widths are gotten from the actual boat as discussed in the text.

Figure 11-6. Fitting the rough blank to obtain the correct taper and bevel on the sides. Leave final shaping until after this operation.

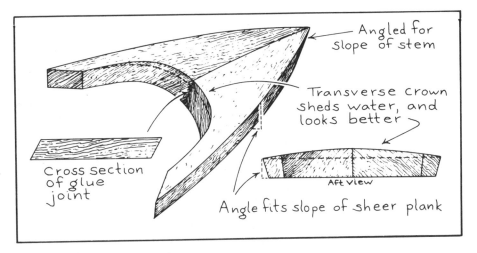

Figure 11-7. Breasthook bevels.

more depending on the twist in the planks. I find it easiest to cut the least acute angle on the bandsaw and plane in the necessary change.

I lay out the cut by finding the actual widths at the sheer for the forward and aft ends of the breasthook. I use the glue joint of the halves as a centerline and measure out one-half of the correct measurement from this, square and true in each location. I connect these points to get my line. Leave the pencil line when you cut, and you will ensure that the breasthook, when fitted, will stand just a bit above the sheer, giving you some excess in which to plane a crown across the top (see below).

You will need to get the correct angle where the "pointed" end of the breasthook meets the stem. It is conventional to make the other end either vertical or inclined a few degrees aft of vertical.

If the inwales meet the breasthooks, you may need to modify the thickness of the side legs to reflect the particular needs of the design you are using. On an open girder rail, for instance, the side legs act as the last spacer block for the rail and need to be the same thickness as these blocks. The inside and outside bevels of each leg should be parallel, or they may be asking the inwale to take a sharp twist in a rather short distance.

Finally, as an aesthetic consideration, the breasthook is usually radiused or crowned across the top rather than being left flat. This radius is transverse rather than fore and aft, and is most easily begun with the breasthook outside the boat. I begin with a scrub plane, then switch to a small rabbet plane for greater control. Finish with the breasthook fitted and glued in place, using a scraper, rasp, or sandpaper to bring the edges flush with the sheer.

Figure 11-8. Cutting the join angle for the inwale in the breasthook leg. No special angle is called for, but around 45 degrees creates a good glue area without making an excessively long joint, which would be harder to fit. Make this cut straight and keep it square to the surface of the breasthook to aid in fitting the inwale.

Figure 11-9. Sawing out the final form of the breasthook after it is fit. A coping saw is a good tool to cut the curve of the after end. This curve is generally beveled toward the bow; that is, the top of the hook is a little shorter than the bottom. A bench vise is used to hold the workpiece.

Figure 11-10. Sawing complete. Note layout lines.

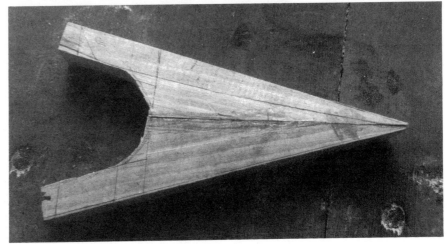

All in all, there is quite a lot of cutting, shaping, and fitting required to install one of these pieces. Generally the aft end of the breasthook is cut in an arc as well as an angle, and the intersection of this arc and the projection of the side legs is an especially difficult point. The bandsaw can't make the full cut without cutting into the side leg a bit, so you'll have to make your cut as far as you can, and finish it off with a sharp chisel. I find it's easiest to cut the side legs on the inside with a backsaw. A coping saw with a sharp blade can do these cutting chores for you, too, with a minimum of fuss.

Figure 11-11. Clamping the breasthook. Small C-clamps hold the legs, a welder's clamp with swivel anvils is forward. Screws (⅝-inch, Number 4, one each side) have been run through the sheer plank to add clamping power and to aid in positioning the piece.

Fitting the breasthook can be troublesome, but one factor is on your side. Because it is wedge-shaped it is hard to remove too much material; the breasthook will just slide in deeper until the gap is filled. It may grow shorter as you progress, but it will eventually fit. It is worth taking the time to make the best fit you can here, both for strength and looks. This is one spot where relying on the gap-filling properties of epoxy isn't the best bet, because too wide a glue joint, especially if the glue has been thickened with silica, will tend to be more brittle than a good wood-to-wood fit. Be careful to keep the breasthook's centerline over the boat's centerline, and not canted off to one side.

I find that a small inspection mirror such as a dentist or a guitar-builder uses is really helpful in letting me see the state of the fit underneath and up at the stem.

I have installed the breasthooks using only glue, but customarily I use a few small screws through the planking and into the breasthook. These can help to reinforce the joint, but their real value lies in positioning the piece and clamping the joint until the glue dries. The screw heads are later covered by the rubrail, so they will not be seen.

Clamping the triangular shape is not easy—there is limited opportunity for purchase and clamps tend to slip. I usually use one clamp from the stem to the back of the breasthook, which pulls the whole assembly into the stem, and a few small C-clamps on the ends of the legs in addition to the screws.

Figure 11-12. Cleaned up, smoothed, and the top rounded.

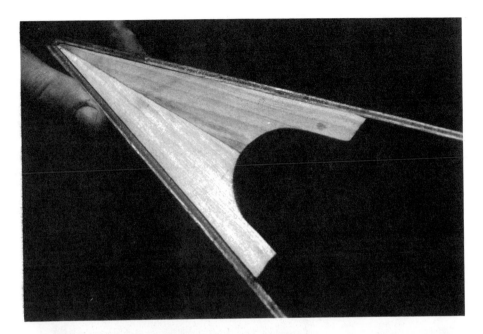

Figure 11-13. Finished breasthook and inwales on the 11-foot canoe.

The preceding comments are mainly applicable to breasthooks in open boats, which need to be "finished" in appearance. If the boat is going to be decked, the breasthook can take the form of two separate knees. This allows easier fitting because there are fewer edges to deal with simultaneously. One side can be fitted first, and then the other side can be fitted to that.

As in the undecked structure, the breasthook parts should be installed somewhat proud of the sheerline, in this case so they can be bev-

Figure 11-14. Finished breasthook. This installation is for an open girder rail (inwale fastened to spacers), so the leg on the breasthook corresponds to the thickness of the last spacer, and the inside surface of the leg is cut at a bevel that mirrors the bevel of the breasthook edge in fitting. If it were arbitrarily cut square, it would make the inwale twist.

eled to fit the deck radius. The deck on top of them will act as a web membrane and supply the missing transverse strength and triangular bracing that two separate knees lack. Alternatively, the breasthook may be dispensed with as in Figure 11–22.

Rails

The primary function of rails in an open boat is to guard against abrasion and give transverse strength and stiffness to the hull. In a kayak, where the deck provides a lot of this stiffness, rails (specifically the inwales) serve more to provide anchoring for the deck. It is a good idea to radius and tape the deck/hull seam at the sheer, and you can dispense with a wooden rubrail altogether in favor of several layers of tape.

Rails generally fall into two types: open or girder style, and solid. The girder type (Figure 11–14) is very strong and also ornamental. It requires more time and materials to build. On my small solo canoes, the girder rails and breasthooks probably account for one-third of the total planking time to make and install.

A rail of solid strips on either side of the sheer plank (see also Figure 2–7) is quicker and easier to put into place, and is still fairly strong. I have a friend who builds small taped-seam canoes in which the only rail is a small-sectioned rubrail of spruce. There is no inwale at all. These boats are very flexible, but are still holding up after a few years of use.

Girder Rails

The first step in laying out a girder rail is to fit a series of evenly spaced blocks on the sheer plank. I measure the distance between the breast-hooks, using the spot where the inwale joint begins as my reference mark. It is customary to leave open the spaces immediately adjacent to the breasthooks. To end up with those two open spaces, you will need an odd number of total units (blocks and spaces combined). The blocks and the spaces will be the same size, somewhere around 4 inches being a good length. This is long enough to glue well but not so long as to be much in conflict with the curvature of the plank. I divide the overall distance by an odd number until I get a good, workable length. For example, say the space between breasthooks is 119⅝ inches (.625 inches in decimal). Twenty-nine spaces would give 119.625/29 which is 4.125 inches. Each space, empty or filled, would measure 4⅛ inches.

I set my dividers to this exact figure, then I step it out on the sheer and adjust if there is some error. There always is, at first. If I get within ¼ inch or so, I'm happy and mark off the points on the boat. You can fudge the last few blocks to cover this amount and it will not show.

I use the divider marks to create the units. It's easy to get confused between open spaces and blocks unless you mark which is which. A pencil line in each space for a block is simple and will be covered up when the block is glued in place.

It's best to glue in the blocks and let them set up, and then fit the inwales afterward. I put the rubrails on last. It is possible to glue the blocks and the rubrails in one operation, but I shy away from this, having learned that bending in the rails changes the shape of a light boat enough to matter. I use a spreader to hold the hull beam to a fixed measurement while bending in any rails, and I leave one inwale clamped in place while I fit the next. The one time I didn't, I got a nasty shock when the last inwale came up inexplicably short after a successful dry fit!

In any case, I like to get the entire breasthook and inwale structure solidly installed before I bend on the rubrails, because they tend to lock the boat into a fixed shape.

Try to install the blocks and rails level with the sheerline, which is already planed true and fair. The curve of the sheer may not fit the straight blocks exactly. If this is the case, install the blocks or rail proud of the sheerline and plane or scrape them to the line later. Do not glue them below the level of the sheer, since this will create a local hollow requiring a lot of planing to remove.

I make up all the rail and block stock at the same time so that the pieces are of uniform dimensions, usually allowing one extra rail in case something snaps. I cut the blocks out of a longer strip using a cut-off jig, and I make extra pieces.

The ends of the blocks look better if they are rounded, or even better,

Figure 11-15. A piece of scrap the same dimensions as the inwale and about 2 to 3 feet long has been clamped into place where the inwale would lie. A small bevel gauge is used to take the vertical component of the angle where the inwale joins the breasthook.

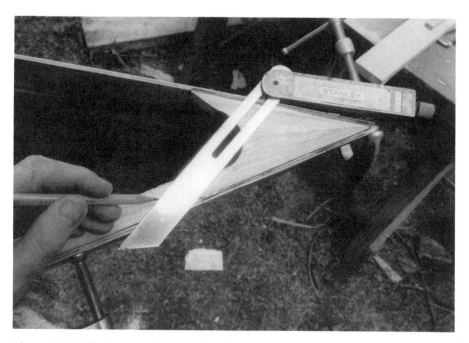

Figure 11-16. The horizontal component of the same joint is taken. The body of the bevel is off the stem but it makes no difference. Any parallel-sided tool or scrap would work. One edge of the blade is aligned with the angle on the breasthook leg (already cut before it was installed), and the other side of the tool is used to transfer this bevel to the dummy inwale. This angle can then be transferred to the actual inwale using a bevel gauge in the usual manner once the correct spot has been found. The clamp in the photo is just to support the body of the bevel square while it is being photographed.

hollowed. I use a router table and a fence to cut the hollows in the ends of the blocks. A slow, gentle feed is needed. A ¾-inch-diameter cutter makes a good radius for ¼-inch blocks.

The end of the inwale is a compound bevel. The best way to get the two angles that make it up is to bend in a dummy rail, a piece of virtually the same dimensions as the actual rail but only about 2 or 3 feet long. This will take enough of the sheer curve to adopt the plane of the inwale. Too short a piece will not do this. The photographs show the procedure. When you have the angles marked on the dummy, transfer them to the actual inwale.

Cutting Inwale Ends for Girder or Solid Rails

Cutting the first end is easy. If you make a mistake you can cut it again, or pare it down. A small plane, such as the No. 90 rabbet by Stanley, a rasp, and a 1-inch paring chisel are my tools of choice for this job.

The next end is harder. You have to cut to a specific length, and there isn't much room for error.

There are two schools of thought as to how to proceed. Some build-

Figure 11-17. Finding the spot. The other end of the inwale is presumed to be already cut, fit, and clamped into place; fitting the first end is straightforward since the critical element of length is not a factor. Use enough clamps so that the inwale is lying right where it will be in the final glue-up. Cut the inwale just a little longer than the final length will be. Clamp it to the sheer plank as close to the other breasthook as you can. The sheer plank is being bent slightly inward by the clamp, showing that the clamp is almost as close as it can get. Mark the inwale and sheer plank of the boat with a pencil tick (a straight, neat line) at the last clamp you use. This is your reference.

Figure 11-18. Now measure from the outside edge of the breasthook leg joint to the pencil tick. This is the short end, or where the bevel will begin. The bevels you gained from the dummy piece are the angles you need to cut the inwale. They are laid out from the point on the inwale corresponding to the distance you just measured from the breasthook to the tick mark. Remember that the tick mark is in the plane of the top of the inwale; lay out your angles from the top and not the bottom of the inwale. If you cut to just leave the lines, you should be within an ace of fitting the piece.

ers like to cut a little long and whittle down. I find, though, that during this trimming process I invariably lose one or both bevels. I like to get the correct length, lay out the proper angles at the right spot, and then cut, leaving just the line showing. Of course this means you have to be sure of your bevels and length, but double-checking and the dummy rail can help here.

How do you get the right length? When one end of the inwale is right, fit it against the breasthook and clamp it into place. Rough-cut the other end so that it is just a little long, but with approximate bevels so that the fit is very close. Now you can clamp the inwale to the spacer blocks at close intervals all the way up, as close to the other breasthook as you can get.

At some point, because of its excess length, the inwale will no longer touch the blocks. Just before this point, where it is still in contact with the blocks, make a pencil mark across both the block and the inwale. Now measure the distance from this mark to the beginning of the inwale joint on the breasthook, or any other reference point you choose.

Measure this same distance from the mark on the inwale forward to find the point where you'll make your cut. This is how the old-timers did it, and it works very well. A folding wooden or a metal rule is the thing to use.

Figure 11-19. Clamping the inwale. Not all the clamps are on yet. Note the use of a spreader to counteract the bend of the inwales and to keep the hull at the correct beam. Because of springback, you might even want to hold the hull slightly wider than its designed beam.

This same technique can apply to any similar situation—a rail next to a plank, or even the length of a plank in a rabbet. It's also the technique to use for fitting a solid inwale.

It's important to keep in mind that in a decked boat the inwale also serves as a support for the edge of the deck. It should be deep enough—1 to 1¼ inches—to offer a good area for the deckbeam to contact. Since the deck will come down at an angle, the inwale will have to be beveled for a good fit. I find it easiest to install the inwale ⅛ to ¼ inch above the sheerline so as to leave material for beveling. (See the discussion on deck beams on pages 132–135.)

The fit of the inwale to the breasthook can be a trying one. Using an inspection mirror can be very helpful here, since it lets you see what is happening to the entire joint, not just the easily visible parts. Sometimes using chalk or a feeler gauge to find the high spots is a great help as well.

Figure 11-20. All clamps on—spring clamps, bar clamps, and C-clamps are all being used. "Too many clamps" is a concept you shouldn't worry about. There are probably 80 to 90 clamps on this 16-foot hull, but you could get by with fewer. Their combined weight is probably 3 to 4 times the weight of the hull, so bracing and shoring will be needed to keep it from distorting under their weight.

Figure 11-21. More clamps. Note the use of plywood scrap (behind boat) clamped to rail to keep the hull from capsizing under the weight of clamps.

The Rubrail

The rubrail (the rail around the outside of the boat) is much easier because it can be put on long and trimmed to fit—no fussy bevels here!

About the only problem is figuring out how to clamp the ends. Clamps do not stick to the converging angles at the stem. Even double-swivel welders' clamps (which hold almost everywhere) tend to slip here. I have used a small machine screw in the waste rail material for-

Figure 11-22. On a kayak, the inwales can simply be brought together in a bevel at the ends, since the entire structure of inwales and deck seems strong enough to make a separate breasthook redundant.

Figure 11-23. The kayak's deck ridge beam (see Chapter 12) further strengthens the breasthook substitute of inwale ends and decking.

ward of the stem to draw the two parts together. I was finally shown an excellent clamping method by a friend who builds ultralight racing catamarans. It offers more control and is easier to manage. Simply place a small C-clamp near the end of each rubrail, with one foot of the clamp on the top face and the other foot on the bottom face of the rail. A clamp so placed will prevent slippage of a larger clamp abutting it on the 'midships side, with one foot on the rubrail's outer edge and the other foot inside the breasthook.

Bear in mind that if yours is a decked boat, the rubrail will go on after the deck is in place.

12. Decks, Cockpits, and Coamings

Decks are what separate kayaks from canoes, although there is a gray area wherein only the subtleties of hull form and paddling style allow distinctions between covered canoes and kayaks.

Buttoned up with a deck and a spray skirt, a kayak is a proper little ship, capable of weathering quite a lot in the way of sea and wind, more than most paddlers would care to experience.

Decks serve several structural functions. They keep out water. They act as web membranes that strengthen the hull in a transverse direction, stopping panting and flexing in the topsides. Finally, they must be able to support the weight of the paddler as he or she enters or exits the craft. Often this last test is the most severe of all.

If a wooden kayak presents special difficulties to its builder, they will probably be in the area of decks. It's usually a fair assumption that building the deck and cockpit will be as much trouble or more than planking the hull.

There are two basic schools of thought in deck design. One holds for high-peaked decks that give good interior volume and water-shedding capability. This peaked configuration is usually limited to or much more pronounced in the forward end of the boat. Rear decks are usually kept much flatter to aid in entering or exiting the boat, both under normal circumstances and from the water after a capsize. The flatter rear surface is also better for carrying a deck load, if this is desired.

The peaked deck creates a lot more windage and resistance which, coupled with a high hull volume, can make for cranky handling when the wind pipes up, especially if the boat is not fully laden. On the other hand, higher decks are somewhat drier in a chop and offer much greater load capacity, which is important on long trips.

The other approach is to use a lower, slightly rounded deck throughout (see Figure 3–3). The low deck may be a little wetter than the peaked one, but I'm not sure how much actual difference this amounts to in a boat with the limited freeboard of a kayak. In return, low decks offer much more freedom from the ill effects of quartering or crossbreezes, to the point of negligibility in a good design. The smaller interior volume may make for a snugger-fitting boat, but again, some people like to have a lot of room inside the hull, and others like to be more securely wedged in.

Based on the use each boat will get, and the type of conditions it will face, there are good reasons for each type of deck. You will have to decide which is best for you.

For the builder, there are definite consequences involved with a choice of either type.

Peaked Decks

In a wooden boat, the peaked deck is a more involved structure, requiring more in the way of an internal framework. Any kind of peak will call for a series of ribs to support it, and possibly a ridgepole as well, although that could be replaced by fiberglass tape, as with the keel.

A light plywood peaked deck will need to go on in pieces—at least one to a side. The cockpit is a funny transitional area where the peak is becoming flatter, or somehow being interrupted. If there is much in the way of angle changes here, it will call for more framing, and probably several more pieces of decking. The rear deck may or may not require several separate pieces plus framing.

Making a light, strong structure with lots of framing is not always easy. Remember that the penalty for weight above the waterline in a boat is loss of stability.

The actual joints between the framing members will be the weakest points, since it will be hard to get adequate gluing surface area. In joining halves of a peaked deakbeam, long scarfs or half-laps are probably best. These can be backed up by plywood gussets (Figure 12–1) or fillet pieces to increase strength.

The areas needing attention will be where the rafter-like beams meet the ridge and where they tie into the hull. These joints will be stressed by the natural tendency of the boat to flex. A crosspiece, like a collar tie in a roof, would serve the purpose, but it would also make the extra volume below the peak quite useless. This means the joints themselves will have to carry the load, with as much help from a triangular gusset or knee as possible. One factor in your favor is that a peaked structure is

Figure 12-1. Deckbeams for peaked decks. The top two sketches show a standard deckbeam comprising two halves joined with a half-lap. The bottom sketch shows a tapered beam, which increases the glue area in the half-lap and obviates the need for a reinforcing gusset at the expense of a slight loss of leg room. This deckbeam shape would result in a 6-inch peak over a 24-inch width.

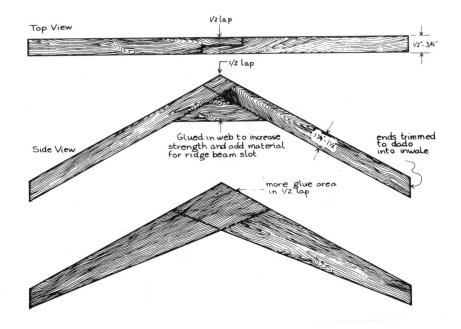

Top View

½ lap

½"-¾"

½ lap

Side View

Glued in web to increase strength and add material for ridge beam slot

1¼"-1½"

ends trimmed to dado into inwale

more glue area in ½ lap

Figure 12-2. Simple glued-up deckbeams. Stock used is about one-inch square. The camber of the deckbeams has been drawn on ¾-inch plywood with six-penny nails to make a simple layout and gluing jig. The angle of the half-lap joint is being marked out. The jig features a centerline, which locates the apex of the joint, and a perpendicular baseline. The deck angles are marked out in relation to the baseline.

virtually self-supporting. Also, once the framework is covered with plywood, it will become quite a bit more rigid.

The plywood deck panels will have to be fastened to the framework, of course, and there are two possibilities here: you can glue the decking down and hope for the best, or you can bed the decks in compound and fasten them with screws, so that any eventual repairs can be more easily performed. The choice comes down to a matter of outlook and whether you are an optimist or a pessimist. My own preference, especially in a multipanel deck, is to glue, because I would be sheathing anyway to seal the edges and strengthen and protect the deck, so deck removal is not going to be practical in any case.

The scantlings for deck framing will depend on what wood you use, the number and spacing of deckbeams, and the height of the peak, to name a few pertinent factors. Hard and fast rules are hard to come by, but it is best to err on the side of strength. Personal experience has shown me that decks wanting in strength are not only hazardous, but are a lot of trouble to fix.

For your framing, use Sitka spruce if at all possible. It glues well, it's very light and strong, and it's just about the strongest material for its weight that you can get.

A good working depth for the ridge and the beams might be between ¾ and 1 inch, possibly up to 1¼ to 1½ inches for the ridge if you choose to use one. These pieces could range from ½ to about ¾ inch thick, as you see fit.

If you can get it, good-quality 3-millimeter Bruynzeel plywood is excellent for the panels. Unfortunately, when I last checked, they had

Figure 12-3. The half-lap in the beams laid out. Sitka spruce is the preferred stock for this type of work.

Figure 12-4. The half-laps cut out. The end of the joint was cut with a backsaw for accuracy and control, and the rest of the job was done on the table saw, using multiple cuts closely spaced and cleaned up with a sharp chisel. To simplify fitting, the laps are longer than they will be in the finished form.

stopped making this thickness, but the 4-millimeter is only slightly heavier and is readily available. It will do quite well in any case.

Looking at other builders' decks is possibly the best single thing you can do. This will show you the variety of solutions to the problem of deck framing and sheathing.

Low Decks

My own personal bias as a designer, builder, and paddler is for low-volume, low-profile boats.

For the builder nothing could be simpler than a low, rounded deck. A few deckbeams make up all the framing. I pick a good curve with not too tight a radius—2 inches over 2 feet, for example—and make a simple bending form. I laminate several spruce beams, lamination producing the strongest beams in these shallow curves. You can laminate one wide beam (I use a 2 × 4 with one edge cut to the desired curve as a form) and re-saw it into two or more narrower beams.

How many beams are needed? I have used just two, one at either end of the cockpit coaming, quite successfully, though this does make a rather flexible deck at the ends. If this bothers you, you can always add another pair or so.

Figure 12-5. Opposing views of the half-laps dry assembled.

Figure 12-6. A pair of deckbeams gluing up. Note waxed paper under the half-laps.

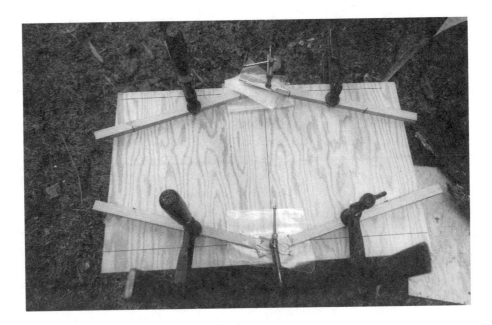

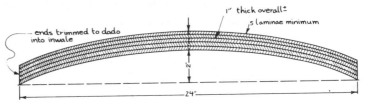

Figure 12-7. A laminated deckbeam for a low deck. Sitka spruce is preferred, although Douglas fir is okay. Make the laminate longer than needed, then trim the ends. This beam shows a 2-inch arc over a 2-foot length. Use the same radius of arc for all deckbeams in a boat, adjusting the lengths as necessary. Recommended dimensions are 1 to 1¼ inches deep by ⅝ to ¾ inch wide.

For low decks, I like to scarf together a big sheet of plywood and put it on in one big piece. This is quick and easy. I do not cut out the cockpit opening at this point, but wait until the coaming is ready. Due to the nature of plywood, you'll be able to get little or no compound bend in your sheet, so you'll need to keep the same radius throughout the length of the deck or suffer all kinds of trouble.

The deckbeams will probably need a slight beveling on their top surfaces; a check with the batten will show you what's needed.

Deckbeam Installation

So far I have talked rather blithely about deckbeams, but haven't discussed the specifics of how they attach or where.

As mentioned in the section on inwales, the deck meets the inwale at an angle that is determined by the radius or angle of the deckbeam, so the inwale will need to be beveled on its top edge to reflect this. Of course the bevel will change slightly along the length of the boat. Putting one of the deckbeams square across the boat will show the required bevel at that spot. I rasp in the correct bevel about every foot or so, and then connect the bevels with a plane. Remember to keep the midpoint of the deckbeam over the longitudinal centerline of the boat while determining the bevel.

After dressing the deckbeams to finished size and cleaning them so that they are ready to install (see the photographs), mark their locations on the inwale, making sure that opposing ends will describe a plane square to the hull centerline. Use the finished deckbeam width to mark out the inwale locations. Rather than just measuring, I cut off a small chunk of deckbeam stock and mark directly.

With a fretsaw and a chisel I notch the inwale, making a shallow dado. It only needs to be ⅛ inch or so deep. The object is to create shoulders that will lock the deckbeams into position, preventing fore-and-aft shifting.

At this point the deckbeam should be cut to fit the dadoes. Note that the curve of the sheer in plan view and the radius of the beam combine to make this cut a compound bevel. Lay a straightedge across the sheer and set a bevel gauge from this to the inwale to get the fore-and-aft

Figure 12-8. Measuring the deckbeam angle at the inwale. Note the clamp and spreader to hold the hull at its designed beam. Deckbeams are centered over the longitudinal centerline of the hull. The cut for this 'midship beam will be nearly square to the longitudinal centerline, but at the ends the deckbeam angle cut will be compound due to the curve of the inwales.

Figure 12-9. Notch the inwale to increase the glue surface area of the joint and provide positive positioning of the deckbeam. The notch needs to be only about one-third into the inwale, approximately ⅛-inch deep.

Figure 12-10. Deckbeam with ends trimmed and glued into notch. Note that the inwale should be slightly above the sheerline to receive a bevel for the deck, and the beam should be slightly above the inwale to be beveled for the fore-and-aft slope of the deck. A pipe clamp holds the inwales tight to the beam while the glue sets; a spreader keeps everything honest.

component of the angle. Use a parallel-sided stick or a square held against the inwale to transfer the vertical angle directly to the beam while you are holding it in place.

Cut the first end and check to see that it is all right. If so, you can make the second cut. I get the position of the second cut by measuring the horizontal distance between the bottoms of the dadoes, straight across the boat, then measuring this same distance across the deckbeam

Figure 12-11. A triangular piece glued into the apex increases the depth of the beam in the way of the ridge beam joint, and generally strengthens the beam. Beams that grow thicker toward the apex are another solution to the same problem. A carlin to support the cockpit rim is visible.

from the outside, bottom edge of the cut I just made. Where a straight line this exact length just touches the outside edge of the other side of the deckbeam, I mark the second cut.

Now the deckbeam should fit tightly in the dado, and it can be glued in. You may want to make up small knees to reinforce the joint. If you have made the rough deckbeam overly long (and you should have), the small scraps from trimming this will work nicely.

As with any job of lamination, a rough laminated deckbeam for a low deck should be longer than the finished piece. This will ensure good glue joints throughout, even though it will be hard to get good clamping right at the ends of the rough blank.

I usually use a bar or pipe clamp to pull the sheer together tightly against the deckbeams while the glue sets up.

At this point, if you're building a high-peaked deck, you'll want to install the ridge beam. The accompanying photographs show the procedure.

Installing a Low Deck

The low deck is best put on in one piece. This is accomplished by scarfing and cutting a deck blank ahead of time, making it 4 to 6 inches wider than the boat and about 12 inches longer if possible. It can be cut roughly to the shape of the sheer to make handling a little easier.

You will need to decide if you are going to glue the deck down or

Figure 12-12. Opposing views of how the ridge beam is notched into the beams in the way of the cockpit.

Figure 12-13. To fit the ridge beam with the intermediate deckbeams, each member is notched about one-half the depth needed. The ridge is slightly above the beams so it can be beveled for the decking on each side of a yet-to-be-scribed centerline.

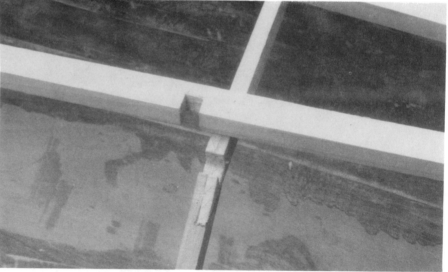

bed it. If you opt for bedding into an oil-based compound, apply a coat or two of varnish or other sealer to the underside of the decking. If you don't, the wood will draw the oil out of the bedding, and it will dry and crack in a year or so. If you use linseed oil remember that it will need several days to dry before you can bed.

Place the scarfed deck blank over the hull, making sure that you have coverage everywhere. Press it down to the sheer (get a helper if you can, or use twine) and trace the shape of the sheer on the underside. It is a good idea to hold the deck in place with a screw or two during this procedure, as it is vital that the blank doesn't shift while you are drawing.

Figure 12-14. Completed deck framing, including the carlins, which define the cockpit area and support the edges of the deck around the opening. See Figure 11-23 for a close-up view of how the ridge beam terminates in the ends.

Figure 12-15. Close-up of the carlin joint where it meets the deckbeam. The carlin is deeper than the deckbeam and is notched around it like an "L" in a simple butt joint. A generous glue fillet strengthens the joint.

Figure 12-16. Another view of the deck framing.

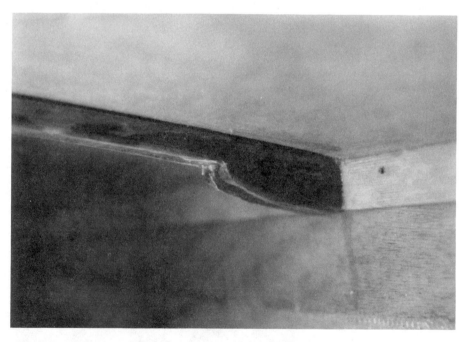

Figure 12-17. Under a low deck, a laminated deckbeam with a knee is used to increase the glue area and make a stronger assembly. This deck is of the flat style, and a pair of beams at either end of the cockpit is all the framing that it uses. The beam is laminated from Honduras mahogany, and I found out that it is too shallow to be properly strong. It's only about ⅝-inch deep and should be about 1 inch or better. Live and learn.

A pair of screws amidships, and possibly another forward, is adequate.

Cut outside the line you have traced, leaving about a 2-inch margin all around. You can cut right on the boat if you're brave, or take the deck off for cutting. Two inches may seem like a lot of margin, but you will find that only a slight misalignment amidships can result in a complete absence of coverage at the bow or stern. Installing the deck involves putting it on and taking it off several times (for marking and drilling), and each time increases the chance of misalignment.

A low deck will have about 2 inches of radius in 2 feet, which can be a fairly tight bend for the plywood decking. I have found that the plywood needs to be screwed down, glue or no glue, since the joint is a hard one to clamp any other way. Placing a screw every 5 to 6 inches uses a lot of screws but is not difficult. You will probably have a sense of how hard the bend is from the preliminary marking episode, and this can guide you as to the spacing needed. The farther apart, the easier your job will be, but too far apart will mean a bad deck-to-hull joint. Pick a compromise distance, and draw lines on the deck for each screw position.

These screws aren't being driven into thin air; you need to know the precise position of the inwale. (You can help by making the inwale of a generous enough dimension to begin with.) Don't trust to chance in finding the inwale. Measure from the edge of the deck blank to the sheer plank at each screw positioning line, or use a try-square as a depth gauge (Figure 12–18). This locates the *outside* edge of the sheer plank. You need to add the width of the plank plus half the width of the inwale to locate where the screw should go. Failure to remember this means that the

Figure 12-18. Installing the deck: Finding the inwale in order to position the screws.

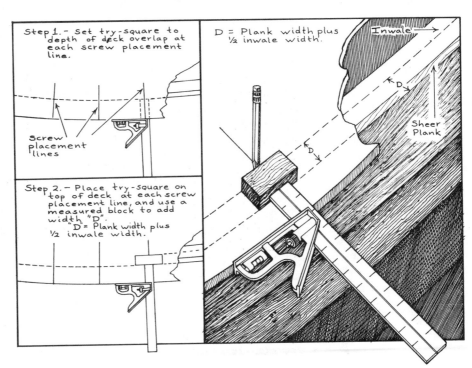

Step 1. — Set try-square to depth of deck overlap at each screw placement line.

Screw placement lines

Step 2. — Place try-square on top of deck at each screw placement line, and use a measured block to add width "D". "D" = Plank width plus ½ inwale width.

D = Plank width plus ½ inwale width.

Inwale

Sheer Plank

screw, when driven, will break through the side of the sheer plank, or perhaps wind up somewhere to the inside of the inwale.

The deck blank needs to be dry-fitted in order to locate the inwale with precision—a rather laborious job because just about all the screws have to be put in. The curve of the deck is effectively tighter in the ends of the boat, where it is narrower, and unless the blank is snugged right down to the sheer your marking will be off, and by a surprisingly large amount.

It is best to start at the point of greatest beam and work forward from there, fastening on both sides of the boat as you go, doing a small area completely before moving on. Then do the after portion. If you start at either end it is too easy to get out of alignment. Remember that this is a dry fit and the screws have limited pulling power (I found Number 4 brass screws—⅝ to 1 inch—to be about right). Do not overtighten them this time around—save something for the final fastening. You can use a triangular awl or a small drill bit for the pilot holes, but don't make the holes too wide where the threads will bite. You may need to just kiss each pilot hole with a fatter bit to give the screw shank clearance, especially if the inwale is thin—say about ½ inch thick. It might be a good idea to stagger the screws on either side of the marking line to avoid lining them all up in the same grain line. I found that having several drills with the correct bits and a counterbore all available at once made the process much more efficient. The 3- or 4-mm plywood is too thin to permit bunging the screw heads. Just countersink enough so they pull down just below the surface.

What this means is that you end up fastening the deck twice, once to fit and once to glue, but that's better than having to install two decks, which a major mistake can call for.

Mark the deckbeam positions on the underside of the deck while dry fitting so that you'll know where to apply glue. Then spread glue on the top surfaces of all inwales, carlins, and beams, and on the corresponding areas of the deck blank. Reposition the blank, and drive the screws again.

You can trim the excess with a saw and a plane after the glue has set up. Then you should seal the exposed edge grain of the plywood at the deck edge, preferably with epoxy. When this has been done you are ready to install the rubrail, which covers the deck edge and caps it off. I like to bed the rails so that they can be removed readily for repairs or replacement. Pre-varnishing the rail before installation saves headaches. An alternative treatment would be to radius the deck-to-hull joint and tape the seam with several layers. The tape then acts as a rail, and an external rubrail can be dispensed with entirely.

The one-piece deck needn't be sheathed, although sheathing will impart added strength and will seal the countersunk screw heads better than would varnish. You will need to fill the countersunk areas with thickened resin, however, to prevent voids under the cloth.

Installing Peaked Decks

The multipanel peaked deck is somewhat easier to install, because several small pieces are more convenient to handle than one large piece. On the other hand, the framing is usually more complicated. Peaked decks don't require the same amount of bend, so the clamping can be accomplished with weights, twine, or shoring, with less emphasis on fussy fastening.

There is the drawback of needing to butt several edges, but you can fit one piece at a time to a previously installed one, thereby reducing the number of variables you have to deal with simultaneously, so it really isn't impossible. Save the sheer (deck edge) for last. This will give you a little margin to fool with if you need it. The multiple-piece deck should be sheathed for watertightness, so some degree of slack in the fits is permissible. This is one place where butt joints are acceptable, but lay them out so they are as short as possible, and then sheathe over them.

If one area looks harder to fit than another put that one on first.

It is possible to install this type of deck with no fasteners. The accompanying photos show some of the clamping methods that will help. You will want to save cutting out the finished cockpit opening until the

Figure 12-19. Installing a peaked deck: Four-millimeter plywood decking is being put on the finished deck framing in quarters for ease of handling. Several clamps along the ridge hold the piece in alignment so that the deck edge can be drawn with a pencil on the underside of the sheet, following the curve of the hull. Cut outside this line by a safe margin to allow for adjustment when gluing all the pieces down. A small (2-inch) margin can also be an aid while using weight or string to glue down the decking.

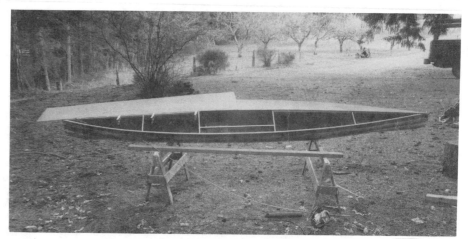

Figure 12-20. The stern half added. Most of the 'midships area will be cut out for the cockpit, with only a few inches of side deck (from the sheer to the carlin, best seen in Figure 12-19) actually butting the forward piece. A butt joint reinforced with tape will be fine, although perfectionists are free to scarf the bow and stern halves if they wish.

Figure 12-21. Clamping a peaked deck at the sheer. Regular clamps are not going to work where the deck and sheer meet. Small screws into the inwale are a possible solution, but a fussy, time-consuming one. Using weight or pressure is a good option, and pressure from a lacing of inexpensive twine is in use here. The hull is blocked up (on the box that the molds were on) so that it can't shift and slacken the twine. Small finish nails are driven into the box to provide turning points for the lashing. Only half the decking is on, so a row of clamps is fastened to the ridge beam to serve as turning points for the upper end of the lashing. Actually, I used several short runs of lashings rather than one long, unwieldy one.

Several of the lashings forward (at the left) are wrapped completely around the hull; if the entire hull were blocked up free of the box, this method could be used throughout. You may need to clamp a light batten along the sheer (using the slight margin you left) to help distribute the pressure from the lashing evenly.

Figure 12-22. Installing a peaked deck: The last pieces of the deck leave no room at all for regular clamps. Here the clamping is done by weight, using a collection of lead blocks, spline weights, and even a gallon paint can. You may need to block up the hull at a slight heel so that the surface of the deck is made flat enough that the weights won't slide off; alternatively, a temporary curbing can be clamped to the 2-inch margin you left in the deck blank. With so much weight on the boat, be sure the hull is shored and braced so it won't capsize. Installing the deck in quarters helps keep the weight manageable. Note that an undersized opening for the cockpit has been roughed out of the deck blank to aid in alignment, clamping (to the carlins), and inspection. It also reduces the length of the butt joint (which shows up well in this photo), and thus makes that joint easier to manage.

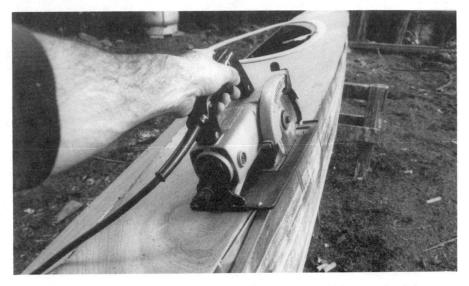

Figure 12-23. The best time to trim the deck edge is after the decking is glued down. Cut as closely as you dare and plane the rest. Setting the blade only slightly deeper than the deck thickness will minimize the damage if you get off course and hit the sheer.

Figure 12-24. The deck edge after trimming. Taping will make the joint a strong, sealed, waterproof affair, but this hard edge needs to be rounded first.

Figure 12-25. The same edge after rounding with a plane and sandpaper.

deck is completely on, but a temporary opening will give you access to the carlins and some of the deckbeams for clamping. If you use weight for clamping, remember to shore up the hull well so it doesn't capsize. You may want to clamp the deck in sections to keep the load on the boat to a minimum.

A radiused and taped rail is really the best solution here, because of the sheathing.

Figure 12-26. Installing a peaked deck: The ridge or deck centerline. This joint will be filled and taped but needs radiusing first.

Figure 12-27. The same joint ready for filling and taping.

Fabric Decks

An alternative decking method is to stretch shrinkable aircraft fabric or canvas over a wooden frame. The frame will present many of the same problems that the peaked deck offered, for the same reasons. Fabric decks are probably better if they are more peaked than flat; certainly then they are less susceptible to the effects of heavy water.

My experience with fabric decks is very limited, but I will pass on what I do know. The cloth cannot solve all your problems. Shrinkage (via a heat gun, hair dryer, or flatiron) is limited to a fixed percentage of the cloth area, so you can't expect huge folds, sags, and bellies to just disappear. You need a fairly tightly stretched deck to begin with. Fabric can conform to quite a few shapes, but it won't take to wildly compound shapes without prior fitting—that is, cutting and sewing. I have learned this from watching airplane builders, who are the real experts in this field.

My friend Don Betts, who has had much more experience with fabric in boats, says that the deck framing required is elaborate and time-consuming. He says he needs a decent fit to the fabric before shrinking, which bears out what the airplane people say. The cloth at the cockpit is cut out with gores and glued to the rim frame in the same fashion as at the sheer.

The fabric can be damaged by too much heat, and airplane builders are quite careful in its application. This care extends to having a temperature chart showing how hot the various areas of their irons are.

After shrinkage, the fabric is treated with paint or aircraft dope. For lightness, this construction has a lot of promise, and it offers the ability to create some exotic shapes. It's worth exploring further for anyone who is interested. Suppliers to home builders of aircraft are the best source of materials and information.

Coamings

The coaming, or cockpit rim, has several functions: It keeps water from spilling into the cockpit, it serves as the lip that holds the spray skirt in place, and it can also be an element in the framing of the cockpit opening. A circular or elliptical shape is best for deflecting water or spray, and this is also the easiest shape to which to attach a spray skirt.

There is a variety of strategies by which a coaming can be made. Rims can be made up of steam-bent members fastened into end blocks, or they can be laminated. Laminae can be arranged to have a vertical, horizontal, or slanted orientation, although the slanted ones are more difficult to form and to clamp.

Vertical Rims

For vertical rims I like to use thin strips that will take the necessary bends without too much strain, because a glued-up stack of laminae can be a real handful, collectively, even when the individual components bend easily. The finished rim should be about ¼ inch thick, and it should take about five laminae to get there. More laminae add more strength. The laminae are table-sawn out of sized stock and should be as thick as will make the sharpest bend without cracking or fighting you. Honduras mahogany is excellent. Spruce is good, but doesn't take sharp bends very well.

The rim will need to be scribed to the camber of the deck to make it

Figure 12-28. Cockpit rim layout. An elliptical shape, with the large end aft, works well. Here the front end is part of a 9-inch circle. Ducks and lead weights are holding a spline in place so the line can be drawn.

fit. This means that the laminae will need to be at least 2 or 3 inches deep to begin with, and must be cut from 2- or 3-inch-wide stock. As a practical matter, I cut my stock to the maximum cutting depth of my table saw blade; you can go no wider because the strips are so thin that you have to rip them out in a single pass.

This rim is best suited to low, rounded decks, or at any rate, decks without too much rocker or camber.

You will need a laminating form, which can be made up of several layers of clear pine fastened to a solid base of ¾-inch plywood or flakeboard. The curves need to be fair and smooth, but only on the outside face, the laminating surface. The actual form should not be too wide or it will interfere with the clamping. Spring clamps are excellent in this application, but the useful sizes can't slip over a form that is much wider than 1 to 1½ inches. When the form is ready it should be waxed heavily so that the rim will release.

Butt joints are fine in the rim laminae. These should be situated on a fairly straight part of the rim (a long side of the ellipse is good) and should be staggered by at least an inch or so between layers.

Getting the correct lengths is simple. Wrap a lamina around the form, clamping as you go, and mark where it overlaps itself. Cut with a fretsaw and re-wrap, only this time put the next lamina on top of the

Figure 12-29. Finished rim layout. Note the centerline and station lines, established to lay out the curve. The spacing of the stations need not be regular. The shape drawn is the inside of the rim— the actual opening. Once this shape is cut out, a second line can be drawn about 1½ inches inside it by running a try-square around the perimeter with a pencil butted against the blade at the 1½-inch mark. The line so drawn establishes the inner face of the laminating form (see Figure 12–30).

first with its butt slightly staggered. Clamp both as you go. Mark the overlap and cut the new piece. Add another layer and repeat. There is a lot of putting on and taking off, clamping and re-clamping. Use enough clamps to press each lamina fully against the form; if you don't, the gap will translate into a difference in length, and the offending piece will be too long when it is fully clamped.

Put on gloves and old clothes, because gluing is messy work. Try not to get glue on the innermost and outermost surfaces of the laminate. These are the finished faces. Spread glue on each piece and stack them with the butts suitably staggered.

Then place the entire bundle on the form and start to work with the clamps. The first few clamps (and the sharpest bend in the ellipse) may be difficult without an extra pair of hands. Press, tap, or clamp the laminae down against the base of the form to keep the edges aligned. Use

Figure 12-30. A laminating form for a vertically laminated cockpit rim. The form consists of stacked layers of ¾-inch pine. Note how the joints are staggered. Fastening the form to a ¾-inch plywood base helps keep it flat, with no twist or sag. Laminae are wrapped around the outer edge, which must be made as fair and smooth as possible. The inner edge (the form is about 1½ inches wide) need not be so perfect, as only the clamps bear on it. A handful of 4 mm plywood pressure pads is in the center. Lots of spring clamps are needed for the laminating.

pressure pads under the clamps to keep the thin strips from twisting or spreading. You may need cauls—pressure pads precisely shaped to fit a part of the curve—if there are hard turns.

If you did the dry-fitting carefully and correctly, everything will come out; the joints will snap into place and you'll be both proud and amazed.

When the rim has set up, clean it with a plane, scraper, and sandpaper, then place it on the deck in the correct spot, making sure it is centered athwartships and not too far forward or aft. Make some marks so you can reposition the rim later. Now cut out an opening in the deck that is a rough approximation of this shape, close enough so you can get clamps on the rim but enough smaller to allow at least a ¼-inch margin for insurance.

Block up the rim with wedges or whatever is handy so that it is level across the boat, and use pencil dividers to transfer the curvature of the deck onto the rim. Be sure to keep the pencil at the same relative angle to the rim all the way around. Don't let the pencil get out of sync with the tracing stylus or you will be transferring the wrong shape in the wrong place.

Figure 12-31. A vertically laminated cockpit rim. The forward and aft ends of the rim are directly over the deckbeams that define the cockpit area. (The forward beam can just be seen.) A lip for holding the sprayskirt is added to the outside of the rim. This type of rim works best on flatter decks because of the height needed in the rough stock to make room for scribing. A rim much over 3 inches high (anything above table saw depth) will be hard to saw out laminae for; the laminae also get harder to clamp as their height increases.

The easiest way to cut out your shape is with a saber saw, leaving the line as a reference. The bottom of the rim should be beveled in accordance with the deck's curvature, a good job for a small plane and rasp. If you work slowly and check often, it will not be difficult.

You will still need a lip for the skirt, because the rim is vertical and not slanted or undercut. Laminate a narrow lip around the top of the rim from thin strips. Some of the coaming material will be just right for this. (You can add the rim before or after you glue it to the deck, but doing it before makes rounding the lip and finishing it much easier.)

Once the lip is in place and you are satisfied with the fit of the rim on the deck, you can glue it into place. Use enough clamps to get a good squeeze all around the joint.

Figure 12-32. The same rim seen from the inside. Note how it rests directly on the deck, being glued to it. It is necessary to scribe the rim to the deck and to plane the changing bevel on the bottom to make a good fit. The opening for the rim is left about ⅛ to ¼ inch smaller than the inner rim diameter until the gluing is done, then it is planed and scraped to fit. For more strength, a narrow ledge for a glue fillet could be left if desired.

When this has set up, use a plane and scraper to make the deck opening flush to the rim. A coping saw will cut away any large areas of wood quite nicely.

If you have sited your deckbeams correctly, the forward and aft edges of the coaming will sit right on top of the beams, which makes a strong arrangement. The rim acts to strengthen the rest of the opening, and the weight of the paddler's body is absorbed by the rear edge of the coaming and the deckbeam.

Flat Rim

If laminating a rim seems like a lot of work, there is a simpler way for the faint-hearted or impatient. You can cut the rim out of thin plywood, like a big doughnut. Four-millimeter planking stock will work, but you will need two or three layers to get adequate strength. Two layers of ¼-inch is good, too.

There is little inherent strength in a flat rim, so the cockpit opening will have to be framed beforehand. It will need to be strong enough to support the paddler's weight. (See the comments on peaked decks at the beginning of this chapter.)

You could use a separate form, but most builders prefer to laminate the rim in place on the framed opening.

The rim can be fastened onto the deck by using thickened glue, filleting, and taping. If there is enough peak or camber in the decks, they will angle away from the rim so that a skirt will fit under it quite well. With a flat deck, though, you may find that you will have trouble getting clearance for the skirt to fit under the rim. If there is any question, lay a straightedge across the deck, or use a sectional drawing to make it clear.

This type of rim is quick and easy, but for me it lacks a certain aesthetic appeal, mainly having to do with the tape and the inevitable crossgrain of the plywood. However, don't let my hang-ups deter you from this simple and workable solution to a knotty problem.

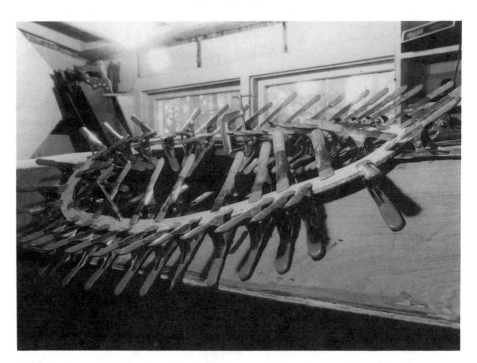

Figure 12-33. A flat, laminated cockpit rim. Two elliptical rims have been cut out— ¼-inch plywood in this case—from the layout in Figures 12-28 and 12-29. These are glued together on the hull to give them a shape consonant with the boat—slightly swaybacked to follow the deck camber. In order to get clearance for the sprayskirt, small blocks of wood are slipped under the rim at the centerline (both forward and aft) and amidships. The rim need only be clamped to the hull at these points to give it the correct shape; the majority of the clamps in the photo are clamping together the two laminae of the rim. Spring clamps are best for this. The clearance above the deck will not be the same everywhere around the circumference of the rim, but this is okay as long as a minimum is maintained for fitting the sprayskirt.

Figure 12-34. A rear view of the flat rim showing the variable clearance above the deck. The rim has been glued into a bed of thickened epoxy near the ridge, and also amidships where it is close enough to the deck to allow this. Fiberglass tape is used elsewhere to make a continuous connection between the rim and the hull. The rim and the underside of the deck at the cockpit edge need to be rounded off to make taping possible. I found that strips cut from my lightest cloth (1.2-ounce) were the best way to start; I reinforced these with heavier tape after the first layers had set. Using short patches (as in taping the stem) may make the work easier.

Figure 12-35. Another view of the same area from the side, showing the tape clearly. Working in a fillet of glue where the tape and the deck meet is a good idea, adding strength and making a tight seal.

Figure 12-36. A view from above. The rounded edges of the rim and deck can be seen.

Figure 12-37. An overall view of the flat rim.

Figure 12-38. Overall view of the deck and rim. A pieced-together deck like this is best sheathed in light cloth, which strengthens and unifies it and guarantees watertightness. The sequence shown here is not optimal. It would be better to cut out the cockpit opening precisely (using the rim you have laminated up in place as a guide) and then glass the deck right up to the opening before installing the rim.

Cockpit Design

We have talked about the technique of building cockpits, but we've given little thought to the underlying concept. Cockpits come in all shapes and sizes. Some are very tight, and others are very large. A smaller opening is usually drier and makes the paddler more "one" with his or her craft. Some people feel that small cockpits are harder to get in and out of, though it seems to me once you've learned to get in and out of a kayak in the first place, there isn't a lot of difference. The dividing line seems to be at the knees. Many people are much happier if they can stuff their knees into a boat while they are already sitting in it, but some boats require that you sit on the rim and slide your knees in as you sit down. Agility, build, and temperament are all factors, I suppose. I always feel like a pea in a shoebox if I'm rattling around in a big, wide cockpit, but other people like the room and the ability to radically change position while underway. Being able to draw one's knees up occasionally is restful and can relieve muscular strain. Again, it comes down to personal preference. The best plan is to try out different boats and decide what works for you.

Most cockpits are raised at the forward end, the better to keep green water away from the paddler. On some boats this rise can be quite pronounced. Likewise, decks usually fall away from the rim, which keeps it drier and makes putting on and taking off the skirt easier. A good, dry cockpit design means that you can paddle in calm weather without a skirt, a practice frowned upon by some, but comfortable nonetheless.

Many people swear by molded seats in a variety of designs, but I've had really good luck with sitting on an old flotation cushion, which has, by now, molded itself to my backside in a rather comfortable manner. The important thing is that you be up a few inches off the bottom of the boat, in case you paddle in cold water, or if there is a little bilgewater. Being raised up a bit also lets you keep your legs slightly bent, which is more comfortable.

Some type of backrest is essential for comfort and paddling efficiency. Everyone's back is different, but in general support of the lower back is the most effective.

In a small cockpit you may be able to use the back of the rim as a backrest, but a bigger cockpit opening means that you will have to rig up some type of backrest, preferably an adjustable one.

It should be hinged or removable so that you have access to the storage space behind it. A simple approach might be to use minimal hardware (possibly home fabricated) for a hinge, and line or shock cord to adjust it. Be creative. The accompanying photographs offer one or two ideas.

Good foot, knee, and possibly thigh braces are essential for transmitting paddling power to the boat, maintaining control in rough water, and for rolling.

Figure 12-39. Backrest configuration.

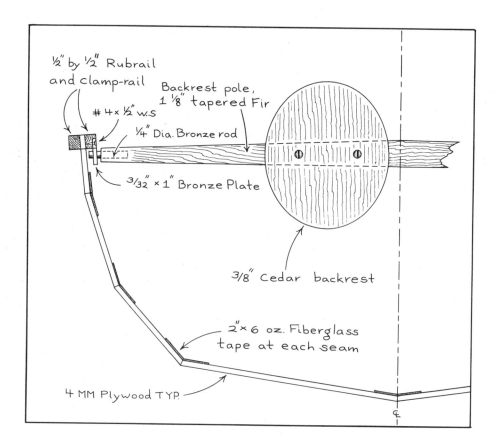

Figure 12-40. Detail of the backrest pads showing how they can be mounted on angle pads to make a more comfortable arrangement. These pads are roughly oval and about 5 inches high. Some people may want higher pads or have other special needs. I have found that generally it is the lower back that needs to be supported for comfort and paddling purchase. (The canoe shown in this and the next photograph is the lapstrake Wee Lassie I used as a model for the 11-foot tack-and-tape canoe.)

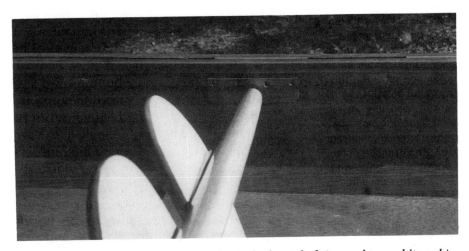

Figure 12-41. Detail of the backrest pads, the backrest shaft (tapered toward its ends) and the bearing plate in which the whole assembly turns, freeing the backrest to give support at any angle. The bearing plate is let into a short (18- to 24-inch) backrest rail of the same material and width but deeper than the inwale, and glued to the inwale's underside. The plate is held with 3M 5200 adhesive bedding compound (which is very strong stuff) and four No. 4 brass screws. This installation is on a highly finished girder-rail canoe. For a simpler single inwale glued directly to the sheer planking, the plate could be let into the inwale itself.

Adjustable footbraces are easy to come by, and do the job quite well. Some low-decked boats almost don't need braces since you can wedge yourself in where you want.

Knee and thigh braces are really just pads placed strategically on the deck or hull. Don Betts—ever innovative—cut two small openings in the deck of one of his boats and placed gasketted canvas patches over them. Properly positioned, these made among the most comfortable and positive knee braces I've ever used.

Bulkheads

Many builders include bulkheads in their boats, and many paddlers swear by them. Their safety features are undeniable—they create watertight compartments in the boat and limit the amount of water that a swamped boat can take on, which makes bailing or rescue easier.

I am not completely sold on their merits, however, especially for wooden boats. This is, of course, personal opinion rather than cold, hard fact.

Bulkheads cut off major air circulation through the hull, never a good idea in a wooden boat, no matter how much, and with what, you have sealed it. If this makes me old-fashioned, so be it, but I have seen my share of cold-molded, "sealed" boats rotting away from the inside out.

Bulkheads do not mean dry storage. You still need to bag your gear. Further, if you use bulkheads it means that you need hatches. Many paddlers seem to love decks strewn with hatches, compasses, fishing pole holders, and all kinds of gear. I much prefer a clean deckline with only a few tie-downs.

Apart from this, hatches add expense and compromise the structural and watertight integrity of the hull. In the effort to attain a useful size, most of the hatches I've seen have sacrificed seaworthiness, and the small screw-on types are ludicrously small. Personally, I'll keep on using airbag flotation and bagging my cargo.

If the real safety benefits of a bulkhead appeal to you, you may want to look into a sea sock—essentially a large waterproof bag that inverts over the cockpit rim and contains the paddler while sealing off remote underdeck areas from boarding seas. This serves the same function as a bulkhead and has been highly touted. Sea socks are commercially available.

Deck Lines

As stated, I do not have a lot of use for deck gear. But you should have some tie-down lines to hold a spare paddle and possibly a chart. Grab lines are also needed.

Bow and stern loops and a grab line along the rail are a good idea, especially if you end up in the water and need to hold on to your sleek, slippery craft. If you predetermine where you want the eyes, you can glue backing blocks of wood or plywood to the underside of the deck for reinforcement before you screw them in. A thin plywood deck may need a bigger area of reinforcement than the size of the eye would indicate. You may need to orient the blocks so they don't interfere with the curvature of the deck as they are installed. If there is a lot of curve, you can shape a block and glue it in after the deck is in place, using gravity, weight, or tiny shores to hold it in place to get clamping pressure. Instead of eyes, a scaled-down version of a yacht's handrail might serve as an excellent source of tie-down points and as a handhold.

A boat full of water is very heavy. If you are calling on your bow and stern loops to take some of this load, make sure that they are adequately anchored. But in all truth, a frameless wooden hull shouldn't be lifted bodily out of the water when it is fully or even partially flooded. It isn't designed for that kind of stress. The better approach is to raise up the boat in a fashion that empties it as you lift it.

13. Finishing

A taped-seam hull is best finished with an opaque paint rather than a transparent oil, varnish, or epoxy. Particularly on a small canoe or kayak, the edges of neighboring tapes will be separated by no more than an inch or two of bare wood amidships, and will converge in the ends of the boat, so a transparent finish would look more silly than attractive. Clear finishes can be pleasing on paddles and on low, one-piece kayak decks, however, and a few general thoughts about finishing will perhaps prove useful.

Types of Finishes

I have had a horror recently of varnish, and to a lesser degree, of paint. Perhaps I've been an exhibitor at too many boatshows, heard too many "oohs" and "aahhs" over a coat of varnish. Many people didn't even see the boat underneath it, whether it was well made or not or even if it should have been made in the first place. I don't care to hear again how "warm" wood is. And heaven help you if there is a run or "holiday" in the finish. No words are spoken, they just touch the offending spot sadly with a finger and turn away . . . but I digress.

Some kind of finish is essential to protect your boat. The range of possibilities is very wide. Your choice could be dictated by such things as looks, cost, work involved, or ease of maintenance. Generally, the glossier and shinier the finish, the more it will cost you in preparation and upkeep.

At one end of the scale are oiled finishes. They have been around the longest; the planks of Greek triremes were tarred, as, for centuries, have been the working boats of Europe and the Mediterranean. Linseed oil has an equally ancient history as a preservative and water repellant.

These are workboat finishes. They do not shine or gleam, and they darken with age and sunlight. But they are effective, reasonably priced, and easily renewed.

Rather than use a commercial oil, I make up my own mixture of linseed oil, pine tar (for body), and turpentine (as a drier). It is very effective, long-lasting, and smells properly salty. It does its job, requires little maintenance, and is easy to renew. It's also dark, dull, and workboatish. Pete Culler had good things to say about this type of finish.

This oil is best applied hot. I do the first coat or two before the deck is on, letting it soak in and then wiping off the excess with a clean rag. Later, I just pour a quart or so into the decked hull and roll it around until everything is suitably coated, wiping down with a rag where I can reach, and using a rag on a stick where I can't.

I have used an epoxy resin coating as an interior finish on several kayaks. My reasoning was that I wouldn't be able to get inside the boat very easily to refinish later, so the more permanent the coating, the better. I have a nagging suspicion, though, that there may be a pinhole gap or a tiny holiday somewhere that the water can get into, but can't get out of. . . . I've repaired enough cold-molded boats to know that this does happen. At least it will be good, pickling salt water and not fresh, but only time will tell.

I have seen some quick and dirty boats that were totally sheathed in cloth and resin, left to be the only finish. I've even built some myself. Ultraviolet rays will break this down eventually, but it's amazing how many years such craft will hold up. But it's wisest to cover this cloth and resin with an ultraviolet-blocking varnish or an opaque paint.

The next step up the scale from oil is the painted surface, which can range from Early Workboat to gleaming and nearly flawless. Paint can be quite attractive and is still much less trouble than varnish. It holds up to sunlight better, and has served boatmen a long, long time.

You do not need to use marine enamel, of course. Porch enamel can give an excellent finish and holds up extremely well. Others use and recommend housepaint. But for the official gloss and the accepted range of colors, marine enamel is the only way to go.

Varnish finishes are at the top of the list. Despite my comments earlier, they are wonderful to look at (although there can be too much of a good thing), but they do require the most preparation and meticulous application.

Being transparent they do not hold up as well to the sun, though they are available in UV-blocking configurations, and they need more frequent renewal to look their best. If varnishes are neglected too long (water stains and the like), there is no remedy but total stripping and refinishing.

There is an ongoing debate over polyurethane varnish versus the old oil-based varnishes. My own experience has led me to side with the latter category.

The polys are harder, but this is not always an advantage. They are less flexible, and thus perhaps less suited to a flexible substrate like thin plywood. They may also be adversely affected by sunlight.

When polys fail they do so in a spectacular manner that calls for total refinishing. Oil-based finishes, by contrast, oxidize layer by layer. Sanding down to a fresh surface and recoating is often an effective remedy.

I once had a small livery fleet, which included boats with oiled finishes, oil-based, and polyurethane finishes. The polys held up the least successfully of all, and the work needed to restore them was the greatest. Perhaps others have had a different experience, but I've been best satisfied with high-quality oil-based products.

Covering Fiberglass

Boats built with glued construction are often totally sheathed in fiberglass, and on such a surface polyurethane coatings—both varnishes and paints—have a much better record for adhesion and durability. Proper surface preparation and application requires a specialized knowledge, though, and asking some questions of a yard painter, a trustworthy dealer, or a knowledgeable owner can help you determine the best methods and materials for your purpose. The two-part coatings such as Awlgrip and Imron are the most difficult to apply, and are perhaps best left to the professionals. The one-part polyurethanes are more user-friendly.

One book that covers this topic extensively is *Fine Yacht Finishes*, by Paul and Marya Butler, published by International Marine Publishing, 1987.

Smart Design: Easy Maintenance

You can make maintenance easier, or turn it into a real chore, simply through small changes in design even before you build the boat. Little, dark corners where dirt can hide, or crevices that won't drain and stay damp, will take their toll despite your best efforts. A sharp edge or a decent radius can make the same detail either prone to drips and sags or a piece of cake. An elaborate molding can be impossible to sand and a generator of drips and frustration.

Proper assembly and prefinishing of certain parts can reduce the time of overall finishing. For instance, some pieces, such as coamings, are best finished with one or two coats before they are glued down, especially if they are to be varnished. Those few coats seal the grain against glue stains and make clean-up a simple task. If you want to save time and trouble, make prevarnishing with a coat or two the rule rather than the exception.

Application

Without going into step-by-step instructions for the variety of finishes that are possible for your glued-construction canoe or kayak, I'd like to give you some tips—pointers that I've found particularly useful.

Proper surface preparation is the key to a good paint or varnish job. Feather all tape edges, as described in Chapter 10, and fill any print-through of the weave with resin. If grinding and hand sanding alone can't provide a fair and smooth surface, use an epoxy fairing putty thickened with microballoons to fill in the nicks and gouges. Finally, sand with progressively finer grits.

Always do your sanding with the grain. This is essential for varnish and all clear finishes, otherwise the tiny cross-grain scratches will show up clearly.

You can never sand enough, but soon enough you will get your fill of it. Wiping some turpentine on the surface will give a temporary gloss so that small scratches and flaws will show up. This is a good way to see how your work is coming along. It's up to you to decide when enough is enough.

You need a clean surface to coat. This means you have to get *all* the dust off. I brush, then vacuum, then dry wipe, and follow this with a turps wipe, followed by a tack rag. Tack rags are commercially available.

You might be able to get away with painting in a dusty area, but it won't work when you varnish. I don't even attempt varnishing in my shop, because just moving around stirs up the sawdust.

You won't be able to do a good job in poor light. Daylight is best by far. You will be hampered by too much heat, cold, or humidity. Paint is more forgiving than varnish, but if you don't have the right conditions, it's far better to wait until you do.

If you use masking tape, take it off right after the last brush stroke so it doesn't stick too firmly. Masking tape can be coaxed to take a curve, or put on in shorter pieces if the curve is too sharp.

There has been a lot written and said about brushes. An expensive badger-hair bristle brush is a sweet thing, but you'd be surprised at what you can accomplish with a foam brush. They don't load up and carry paint the way a bristle brush does, so the technique is different. You can't brush out your work as long without reloading. But they do work, especially on flat surfaces. Best of all, there's no clean-up. Just throw them away. If that disturbs you from an ecological standpoint, remember that this means fewer solvents get into the ecosystem as well.

Paint out of a can is usually too thick. Thick paint is a hideous thing—it wants to run and sag, it's prone to brush marks, and it is more fragile when dry than several thin coats would have been. There are a few excellent conditioners available. Penetrol is one of the best for marine enamels. Thinning with turps will *not* achieve the same effect. When thinning polyurethanes or alkyd enamels modified with polyurethanes, stick strictly with the manufacturers' recommendations.

I like the paint to be so thin that it almost drips like water off the stirring stick. Almost, but not quite, or it will be *too* thin. Experiment by adding conditioner and brushing out a small test patch, either somewhere hidden or on a piece of scrap. Different paints, even different colors, from the same manufacturer will all call for differing amounts of conditioner.

Don't ever varnish right out of the can. Pour what you need into a secondary container and keep the source clean and free of bubbles.

I like to do the same with paint. For small boats, a 6-ounce plastic cup may be just the right size. One-gallon milk jugs that have been cut down (leaving the handle on) make excellent paint buckets or clean-up pails. I haven't bought a paper bucket in years.

Punch some holes in the groove that the lid of the paint can fits into. This way any paint that gets into the groove can drip back down into the can, instead of down the sides and all over your hands.

Maybe it's superstition, but I take a deep breath and then exhale into a paint can before I cap it. The carbon dioxide displaces the oxygen, and I find that skimming over is not a problem until the very bottom of the can. Use old pantyhose to strain any skin, dirt, or grit out of a previously opened container. It works as well as any filter.

I won't go into great detail on the mechanics of brushing paint out. It's really just a matter of learning to hold the brush at the right angle, and knowing how much or how little paint to apply at once. Each paint, each brush is different. Learn to observe.

Remember to keep a good wet edge, and always be on the lookout for drips and sags—not only where you are working, but where you have been as well. They have a way of magically appearing. Sight from different directions so that light catches the surface in different ways. Brush out your work, but not to the point where it looks like the furrows of a plowed field. Any surface will flatten itself somewhat, but don't use that as an excuse to wreak havoc.

Painting and varnishing is an art. In addition to reading about the technique, it's a good idea to watch someone who knows what they are about. Such people are not that hard to find. Their boats give them away. If that isn't enough, just look for the ones who don't have paint all over their clothes and hands while they are working. You'll spot them.

Maintenance

Maintenance is a key word with wood boats and finishes in general. People assume that a wood boat requires massive amounts of yearly maintenance, spelled D-R-U-D-G-E-R-Y. I am not here to debate the case with big boats, especially decked craft, but a small canoe or kayak need not be a yoke around her owner's neck.

The difficulty of upkeep may be determined by three questions: Can it be cleaned? Can it be sanded? Can it be recoated?

Keeping things clean can reduce overall maintenance by an amazing amount. Dirt, especially salt crystals, is like a rough grade of sandpaper and can quickly scar a finish. My standing policy is to wash off a canoe or kayak after every use—and I rinse my feet off before I get in. Soap and water from a hose work best, but just a sponge and a bucket of fresh water is fine. I either chamois the boat dry, or let the sun do the work, which is a little spottier. This protects the paint and varnish from grit and keeps it healthy-looking. Sponging every inch of the hull puts me in contact with all of it and allows a quick inspection for any new nicks or deep gouges.

I have a three-year-old canoe that has been used by many, many people, not all of whom were knowledgeable about the respect due any boat. It is the veteran of several boatshows, even more hands-on demonstrations, and many, many paddling trips. But it still looks good enough to turn heads and reel in the interested onlooker. This is due to that wash-down policy. The equation I use is that five minutes a day is better than five days each spring.

Can it be sanded? Anything can be, I suppose, but some designs are easier than others. In this respect, there is nothing to equal frameless construction. Anyone who has tried to sand between closely spaced lapstrake frames knows what I mean.

Varnish and paint, if kept clean, should not require major refinishing except at widely spaced intervals, which can vary depending on a lot of factors, most of which you can control.

If the boats are in decent shape, and they should be for quite a few years, a light sanding will expose a fresh surface for any touch-up. Try to take off about as much as you put back on to avoid an ever-thickening buildup.

I find that I can do such a sanding, using 220-grit paper, in about an hour for the interior and exterior of an 11-foot frameless canoe.

Can it be recoated? Again, frameless construction holds an advantage. Good, long, uninterrupted brush strokes can save a lot of time by the job's end.

Some finishes take to recoating better than others. Polyurethane varnishes seem to fail all at once and need removal and redoing rather than recoating. Their hardness and ability to clog paper doesn't make sanding them much fun either, not that regular varnish is much better.

Fiberglass or plastic canoes and kayaks do not require sanding or painting but will deteriorate rather quickly if proper care is not given. Gelcoat repair is difficult and not always successful. Delamination of layups can occur if water penetrates the gelcoat. My own feeling is that a properly cared-for wooden boat will give a long service life to the owner, along with excellent appearance, whereas a glass boat can begin to show her age in not too long a time.

No matter what type of finish you have, a roof over the boat to keep off the sun and the elements can add years to its life. The small, light boats we're building aren't intended to remain on the water, and it's easy enough to store them under some ceiling joists or rafters with slings. Or, you could build a simple rack with a roof. Whatever you do to keep the boat off the ground, adequately ventilated, and out of the elements will be well worth it.

14. Paddles

H ere is a subject guaranteed to raise controversy. There are many types, styles, and lengths of paddles, and everyone is sure that his own particular choice is the only right one. Since a double paddle is the only logical choice for kayak or solo-canoe paddling, we will limit our discussion to these.

Choosing a double paddle for yourself will involve many factors. The length of your arms, your flexibility, your strength, your stamina, and the condition of your joints all need to be considered—not to mention your paddling style and the beam of your boat.

Length and Weight

If nothing else, most people agree on the fact that ocean touring calls for a longer paddle than whitewater. The normal length for a double paddle is about 8 feet, with 6 or so inches on either side for individual variation. Longer paddles have a slower stroke rate, good for touring because it usually calls for a long, steady output of energy rather than spurts of concentrated, furious activity.

A longer paddle gives a little more leverage and control for draw strokes and turns, which can be helpful when turning between waves for course adjustment.

But length is not the only factor. Think of the paddle as a pendulum. The blade, being at the end, develops the most speed and inertia. If the blade and the throat are too heavy, it takes more force to accelerate and decelerate this area. That means more energy and strain, which results in fatigue. This is not an absolute, of course, because it works through the filter of your body and your muscles, but it is an active principle, nonetheless, and affects the relative performance of different paddles for the same paddler. This is why two paddles of the same length and weight can feel utterly different.

I started with a paddle that was about 86 inches long but found that it required a high stroke rate, and that the out-of-water blade rose quite high in the air—almost vertically, in fact. This was not good in a breeze. It also made it a wet paddle, one that splashed and dripped on me unmercifully. Making a 96-inch paddle improved the situation on all counts, but I was even happier with a length of 106 inches. Many people will gladly tell you that this last figure is too long. What they really mean is that it is too long for them.

My current paddle of choice is about 105 inches long. There is no reason for the lost inch—it just worked out that way. I back this up with a store-bought breakdown paddle (one with a joint in its middle, enabling it to be broken down into two pieces) that is 101 inches long. Because of its weight and blade design, the longer one is decidedly more comfortable to use.

Some paddles are just too heavy. Swinging all that mass around at the end of a long lever isn't much fun, and a day of it can be a real trial, not only to your arms and shoulders, but to your hands as well.

On the other hand, I have run into some that were just too light—they felt as if they were going to fly out of my hands into the wind at any moment.

Absolute numbers can be misleading, but a good modern paddle need not weigh more than a couple of pounds. What really counts is the balance and feel of it. Don't just hold it statically. Swing it in a mock stroke and see how it starts and stops. If a paddle doesn't feel right when you pick it up, chances are that it won't improve after a long day of paddling.

Feel

We have touched on the dynamic feel of a paddle—how it swings and moves. In addition, many people like a little spring in the shaft. This gives your muscles some cushion, gives you some feedback in your stroke, and makes the paddle feel a little more alive in your hands. A little bend doesn't seem to rob you of power, since what you lose at the start you get back at the end. Too much bend, though, will take force from your stroke and keep you thinking that the shaft will break at any moment. How much feel, if any, you want in a paddle is a personal choice.

Grip

Most paddles have a shaft diameter of 1⅛ to 1¼ inches. This is not just for strength. Too small a shaft diameter can make for a cramped, awkward grip that is surprisingly tiring. You may not even notice how hard you are gripping until the cramps set in. The extra muscular strain won't be confined solely to your hands, either, but will extend to your forearms as well.

With a well-designed paddle—that is, one with good balance and no flutter—your upper, non-power hand should not need to grip the shaft at all. You should be able just to cradle the shaft between your thumb and fingers during the return stroke. Relaxing your grip like this can help combat fatigue and increase endurance. If your paddle doesn't perform well enough to allow this, look for one that will.

Shafts are usually round in the center, but oval closer to the throat where you grip them. The oval makes the shaft more comfortable to grasp, helps resist rolling, and provides a tactile indicator of blade angle. For feathered paddles, this can be especially welcome.

Paddle shafts of aluminum are almost always padded or taped for comfort, since they can get quite cold. Composite or wood shafts do not require this treatment.

Wood shafts are usually varnished, but I leave the grip area on my paddles bare. A varnished surface is a good blister raiser, especially when wet. I find that a smooth, sanded surface is more comfortable, and oil from one's palm seems to give enough protection. Lots of people will disagree with this—I get stares at my paddle all the time—but I'm happy with it. Look at a good pair of oars. The old-timers who *had* to row never varnished the grips on their oars. They left them unfinished.

Blade Design

Blade design is related to overall length, and really cannot be looked at separately. Generally, the longer the overall length of the paddle, the longer and narrower the blade. A long paddle with a slalom-type blade—short and wide—would be a nasty thing indeed for ocean touring, requiring a lot of muscle to move through the water and probably being untamable in a breeze. It is important to realize that the lessons learned from whitewater do not always carry over to ocean touring, because the conditions are very different.

Of vital concern in blade design is stability. A blade that "flutters" and weaves during its power stroke is very tiring to use, and is not capable of giving you the instant control you may need. All paddle-builders have their own theories, as witnessed by the variety of designs, but a few general principles seem to emerge.

Distribution of area on either side of the shaft is a significant factor. Since the paddle does its work at an angle, and is not even completely submerged at times, an asymmetrical shape seems to do a better job of balancing areas.

Blade configuration plays a key role. Dihedral blades, which are set on a slight angle on either side of the shaft so that the entire blade forms a shallow *V* with the shaft at the apex, seem effective. Of course the angle has to be right, and more is not necessarily better.

Spoon blades curved laterally as well as longitudinally can also be effective, but if the curve is wrong it will aggravate problems rather than help them. Using a spoon blade at the wrong angle of attack can lead to a diving blade and a possible upset. In this they are less forgiving than a flat blade.

Flat surfaces seem to be better suited to narrow rather than wide blades in terms of reducing turbulence and flutter.

Finally, tip design can have a marked effect on the turbulence generated, and hence on the stability exhibited during the power stroke. Whitewater blades are relatively short and wide, which is good for river situations in which you need short spurts of high power, and for bracing in aerated water. They may be sized roughly 10 inches wide and 14 inches long. A "standard" touring blade, by contrast, is usually about 7 inches or a little less wide, and about 18 inches long.

Other paddlers (myself included) have found they prefer the long, narrow Eskimo-style blade, whose typical dimensions might be 4½ inches wide and about 27 inches long.

Although the last two blades may seem quite different in size, their respective areas are close—126 inches for the touring, and 121.5 inches for the Eskimo. The whitewater blade, on the other hand, is a whopping 140 inches.

The similar areas develop about the same thrust, but do it differently. A long, narrow blade has more "slip," to use a propeller analogy, mainly in high-torque situations such as getting underway. This slip (which should not be viewed only as inefficiency) has the benefit of cushioning the paddler's muscles and joints on each stroke. Such a blade will take a little longer to accelerate a boat to cruising speed. At that point, though, the effect of slip is negligible, since less torque is needed to maintain speed, and the narrow blade seems at no disadvantage in keeping the pace, perhaps even taking slightly less effort.

Setting such a blade at the end of a longer shaft seems to make up for the lack of absolute power. In practical terms, I have never found myself at a disadvantage when cruising with others who were using more conventional paddles.

Out of the water, narrow blades are less affected by the wind. The longer shaft means that the returning blade (the one going forward) can be held lower to the water, which is a boon when the wind pipes up.

Some people feel that a narrow blade is a disadvantage for bracing, but my own experience is to the contrary. That the narrow blade has been used in the Arctic for thousands of years cannot be merely a factor of habit or lack of proper materials, as some people believe. It is a blade that has stood the test of time.

Feathering

Whitewater kayak blades are feathered—set at an angle of about 75 to 90 degrees to one another so that the out-of-water blade is more or less parallel to the water's surface. This cuts down on wind resistance and the effects of waves or spray.

The practice of feathering was carried over into ocean touring, but is recently being challenged. One problem is that it seems to be a major cause of tendonitis in wrists and elbows as a result of the constant rotation and counter-rotation it requires. In a six- or eight-hour day, a lot of extra movement and pressure is carried by a few joints.

To combat tendonitis, standard-paddle users tried the dodge of using a breakdown paddle that can be feathered for either right- or left-hand control, or even positioned for no feather at all. This allows the burden, if any, to be shared by both arms. One disadvantage of such a scheme is that if an instinctive brace is needed, the paddle may not be set up in the most familiar configuration.

Another solution is to use blades feathered at less than 90 degrees to one another. Reducing the degrees of rotation of the wrist will go a long way toward reducing strain. A rotation of 75 degrees is often used. Just how far you can go, and what is most effective, is a subject for debate and experimentation.

Another problem with feathering is that high winds tend to make the paddle want to spin, since the faces of the blades are set up like a crude turbine.

Eskimo blades are never feathered, and I have found that the long, narrow blades are controllable in strong, gusting winds. This seems to be the experience of others who have tried them as well.

Build or Buy

There are a lot of beautiful, bright, shiny paddles on the market, most of them backed up with some very impressive advertising copy. So why would anyone want to build his own paddle?

Perhaps it's arrogance, but in trying what's available I've found that

Figure 14-1. Paddle blade and shaft configurations for building. I think the leaf-tipped blade is more stable in use than the conventionally rounded design.

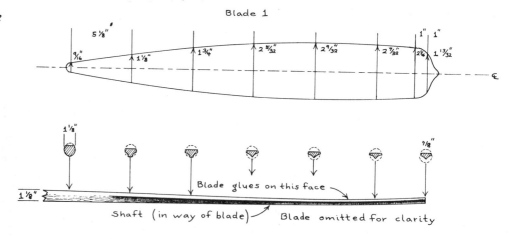

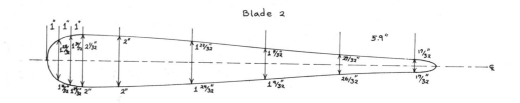

I could build as good or better a paddle in my shop, with only a few exceptions. There, I've said it.

But let me qualify a bit. The paddle I build suits me and my style. It probably won't suit everyone, and the general design and method I've worked out is suited only for my favorite type, the long, narrow Eskimo blade. This is not a whitewater paddle, nor is it intended to be. Trying this same method with a wider blade will lead to loss of performance, feel, and strength.

One very practical aspect to making your own is that you can use planking scraps and common lumberyard materials. For about $8.00, I end up with a paddle that I prefer over commercial varieties that cost $100 and up.

The main ingredient is a 1⅛- or 1¼-inch fir closet pole from the lumberyard. Try to pick a piece without a lot of spiral grain. You'll need to set the blades so that the power stroke isn't trying to lever open a grain line; getting it right at both ends can be hard if the grain turns too much.

In this technique, the pole is cut to length and the blades are glued on. I run the pole down almost the full length of the blades to stiffen them, and to get glued surface area.

I bandsaw a flat in the pole at each end, cutting in only one-quarter to one-third the diameter of the pole in order to preserve its strength. It's important that these flats be in the same plane relative to one another, and that they not be situated in such a way that a power stroke could open up the grain. (This is the major way that a paddle of this kind seems to fail.) I snap a chalkline against the shaft to align the flats and to give me a means of aligning the blades when I glue them on. After cutting the flats, I smooth and true them with a plane.

The blades themselves are fashioned from scraps of 4-millimeter plywood left over from planking. I know this seems almost criminally simple, but they work very, very well.

Now comes the catch. Paddlemaking is black magic. Each piece of

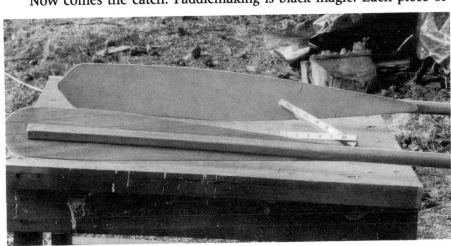

Figure 14-2. Two simple-to-make paddles (blades 1 and 2 from Figure 14-1). The power face shows in the rearmost, the back face in the foremost. The blades are 4-millimeter Bruynzeel plywood (planking scraps), and the shafts are basically 1¼-inch fir closet poles tapered and planed as per the text. Of all the paddles I own, I probably have put the most miles on the leaf-configured one shown here.

Figure 14-3. Same paddles, different view.

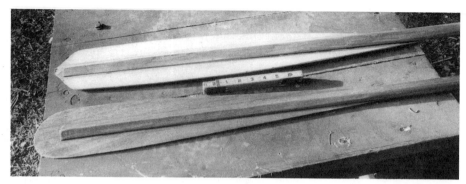

Figure 14-4. The upper end of the blade, showing also the start of the sawn flat in the shaft that serves as a gluing surface for the blade. This flat can be slightly dished if a somewhat curved blade is desired. Use a thickened epoxy (the gap-filling type) for glue. No screws are necessary.

fir is different, especially in its elasticity. I use a plane and a spokeshave to work some taper into the shaft, working out from the center. I bend it against the floor to test the spring and check the swing of it to see how it feels. I balance it on my finger to see that the weight is evenly distributed.

I try to get it as light and as limber as I can without sacrificing strength. You may have to break a few before you learn how far you can go. I did.

How do you achieve the right balance? Try your paddle in actual use and then shave it a little more. Be cautious—you can always take off material, but getting it back on is not so easy! Obviously, too limber a paddle would be a disadvantage, and if it's too floppy, it's not very strong either.

Keep in mind that there are two kinds of bend you can create in your paddle—curvature of the shaft as a whole, and curvature of the blade by itself. The shape and size of the shaft controls the first, while the shape and size of the spine running down the blade controls the latter.

A little curvature taken by the blade during your stroke seems to give it a little bite and make it more efficient, although I would be hard-pressed to prove that with numbers.

I always taper the shaft as it runs down the blade, both in height and width. First I plane the original half-round shape into a triangle, and then I use a gouge to hollow out the sides of the triangle. This retains maximum strength in the spine, while making it as light as possible. You

Figure 14-5. The end of the shaft. The shaft is carried down the blade for strength. Note the triangular section, for minimum weight with maximum strength. More taper at the end of the shaft would be acceptable.

can experiment with blade shape at will. The low cost of materials makes such research painless and fun.

I find that the shape of the tip itself is important. In a pair of otherwise identical blades that I own, the leaf-tipped one is more stable than the conventionally rounded design. You may want to try some of the old Eskimo shapes. I don't think their purpose was purely decorative, at least not in all cases.

Beyond . . .

Beyond plywood paddles are carved ones. My favorite paddle of all time was an Eskimo design carved out of a spruce 2 × 6 bought in a local lumberyard for about $2.00. It was just under 9 feet long and very light and flexible. It was clearly intended to propel a light, easily driven hull. The blade design was virtually the same shape and dimensions as Blade 1 in Figure 14–1, but it had a marked diamond-shaped section with a pronounced center ridge and leaf ends. It was too flexible really, being pared down too much in the throat, and it ended up getting broken by someone who didn't understand the kind of treatment it needed. (That was a black day.) However, it had shown me what could be achieved with basic materials and a few tools. I used a circular saw, a drawknife, a spokeshave, and a bent gouge to make it. I did it in a friend's backyard, miles from my shop, using a stump for a workbench.

The point is that if you decide to build paddles you can do an excellent job with little effort and a low cost. The plywood ones are quite fine, and a good carved one is without peer.

These general directions should be enough to start you off. The rest is gained from experience—in using what you have made and in making more. Each boat and every paddle will come out a little better than the last as your skill and understanding increase. Good luck, and have fun!

A. Sources

Books

Adney, Edwin T. and Howard I. Chapelle. *The Bark Canoes and Skin Boats of North America.* Washington, D.C.: Smithsonian Institute Press, 1983.

Highly recommended source of plans, drawings, and photos. It also contains a variety of information about use, construction and lore for a wide range of canoes and kayaks.

Atwood, Manley. *Rushton and His Times in American Canoeing.* The Adirondack Museum, New York: Syracuse University Press, 1977.

An excellent account of the heyday of American canoeing. Full of valuable information and worth getting just for the appendices, which include offset drawings for seven canoes (including the Sairy Gamp and Wee Lassie).

Brower, Kenneth. *The Starship and the Canoe.* New York: Harper & Row, 1983.

An insightful exploration of the evolving, contradictory visions of George Dyson, builder of baidarkas, and his father, a renowned physicist.

Dyson, George. *Baidarka.* Edmonds, WA: Alaska Northwest Publishing Company, 1986.

A unique and wonderful book! Part 1 is a history of the Aleut baidarka in text and contains old drawings, etchings, watercolors, and photos. Part 2 features a luscious pictorial covering modern baidarka voyaging in all its glory. There are also details for the construction of a modern replica built with aluminum tubing with a fabric skin.

Gardner, John. *Building Classic Small Craft, Volume 2.* Camden, ME: International Marine Publishing Company, 1984.

Contains an excellent section on canoes and includes drawings and offsets.

Hill, Thomas, with Fred Stetson. *Ultralight Boatbuilding.* Camden, ME: International Marine Publishing Company, 1987.

Good source material on another way to build light plywood boats. Excellent photos of methodology.

Zimmerly, David. *Gajaq.* Juneau, AK: Division of State Museum, 1986.

This is an exhibition catalog that's actually a self-sustaining book covering the kayaks of Siberia and Alaska. It contains a wealth of information, drawings, and photos about the use and construction of these kayaks, paddles, and related gear. It also contains many of Zimmerly's excellent drawings, including offsets. Miss this one at your own peril, although it may be out of print and difficult to find.

There were a lot of canoeing books published in the early 1900s that deal with canoes, canoe trips, canoe building. Many were written from a *Boy's Life* perspective (healthy, moral stuff for boys to do), but they have good material in them, including plans and how-to instructions. They can be found cheaply at attic sales, used book outlets, etc. Worth keeping an eye peeled for!

Magazines

Sea Kayaker is an up-to-date quarterly magazine covering kayak voyaging and gear. It has presented some design analysis and usually has historical material as well. (Sea Kayaker, 1670 Duranleau St., Vancouver, B.C., Canada V6H 3S4.)

Canoe presents a wide variety of articles on equipment, technique, and travel for canoeists and kayakers. (*Canoe*, P.O. Box 10748, Des Moines, IA 50349. Tel. (800) 678-5432.)

Plans

David Zimmerly has done excellent drawings of Arctic skinboats as part of his work as an Arctic ethnologist for the Canadian government. His plans are available at The Baidarka Historical Society, formed by a group of kayak enthusiasts with a strong Aleut baidarka focus. They are maintaining an archive of plans and related materials. There is a strong boatbuilding contingent in the B.H.S., and they seek to publish material that reflects this interest. (The Baidarka Historical Society, Box 18, Belcarra Park, R.R. 1, Port Moody, B.C., Canada, V3H 3C8.)

Materials

This list is by no means complete. Local sources of supply for these and other excellent materials exist and are worth tracking down. For the isolated boatbuilder, UPS can open up wide horizons and many options. Reading the advertisements in *Fine Woodworking*, *WoodenBoat*, and *Small Boat Journal* is a good way to see what's available and who has it.

Epoxy Glues:

Chem Tech, 4669 Lander Road, Chagrin Falls, OH, 44022. (216)248-0770

Gougeon Brothers, P.O. Box X908, Bay City, MI, 48707. (517)684-7286

System Three Epoxy, P.O. Box 70436, Seattle, WA, 98107. (206)782-7976

Sheathing, Tape, Etc.:

Defender Industries, 255 Main Street, New Rochelle, NY 10801-0820. (914)632-3001

Fasteners, Paints, Fiberglass (Tools, Materials, and Supplies), Any Boatbuilding Needs:

Jamestown Distributors, 28 Narragansett Avenue, P.O. Box 348, Jamestown, RI 02835. (800)423-0030, (401)423-2520

Plywood:

Boulter Plywood Corp., 24 Broadway, Somerville, MA 02145. (617)666-1340

Evensaw, 5881 Highway 20, Port Townsend, WA 98368.

Floundry Bay, 3rd and O Street, Anacortes, WA 98221. (206)293-2369

Frost Hardwood Lumber, Market & State Streets, San Diego, CA 92112. (619)233-7224

Harbor Sales Company, 1400 Russell Street, Baltimore, MD 21230. (301)727-0106

Hudson Marine Plywood Co., P.O. Box 1184, Elkhart, IN 46515. (219)262-3666

Maurice Condon Lumber, 260 Ferris Avenue, White Plains, NY 10603. (914)946-4111

Hand and Power Tools:

Garrett Wade Co., Inc., 161 Sixth Ave., New York, NY 10013 (212)807-1155

Japan Woodworker, 1731 Clement Avenue, Alameda, CA 94501 (415)521-1810

Seven Corners Ace Hardware, 216 W. 7th St., St. Paul, MN 55102 (800)328-0457

Woodcraft Supply Corp., 41 Atlantic Avenue, Box 4000, Woburn, MA 01888. (617)935-5860

Woodworkers Supply, Inc., 11200 Menaul N.E., Albuquerque, NM 87112. (505)821-0500

B. Experimenting with Existing Canoe and Kayak Designs

Modifying an existing design is neither fish nor fowl. It is not outright design work per se; you are really building on another design as a foundation, but the elements of choice, intuition, and distillation of experience are all present. It can range from the sublime to the ridiculous, depending on how far you distort the boat from its original concept. Modifications work best in moderate amounts, seasoned heavily with experience. Creating an extensive facelift for a design you are familiar with only on paper may not be doomed to failure, but it is an exercise with little basis in reality. The best modifications come after real familiarity with the original. In this appendix we'll look at the effects of modifying canoe and kayak shapes, and discuss some procedures for "doodling with designs" that will work no matter what building method is employed. In Appendix C we'll look more closely at adapting designs for tack-and-tape construction.

What to Change

Most modifications involve some type of scaling up or down of the boat. Length and beam are favorite targets for this sort of activity. A sense of proportion is important. A solo canoe may not be the best starting point for the creation of a six-man war canoe.

One important point to remember is that length and beam do not change by the same factor. For instance, if you decide that a 10-foot canoe would suit you better at 12.5 feet, you have increased the length by 25 percent. But you may find that you don't wish to change the beam at all, or only slightly (about 1 inch up or down). A 25 percent increase in beam could take the boat from 26 to 27 inches to 32.5 inches, which is really too wide.

With canoes and kayaks, the acceptable range of beam is pretty narrow, and unless you are thinking about widening a narrow skinboat from the Arctic (they're usually only 19 inches), beam is a dimension that you'll want to be careful about changing radically without good reason.

This means that lengthening or shortening such a boat really boils down to drawing out or compressing its waterlines, making the curves easier and longer or sharper and tighter. The rate of change in these curves may be what's different, rather than some absolute numbers.

Sometimes just changing the spacing of the molds is

all you need do to change the length of the boat; everything else stays the same. This technique was used by traditional builders.

In keeping with our realization that no single part of a boat is isolated from the rest, we will need to examine freeboard, rocker, and height of the ends as we change length or breadth.

Freeboard is a slippery animal to pin down. It is related to dryness of ride, and to some degree, to safety in rough water, but maybe not as much as some people would think. It is also related to windage, weathervaning, and looks. The amount of freeboard needed both forward and amidships is in part determined by the flare of the hull and its ability to rise to oncoming seas, which is a function of her sections. In a canoe, the load capacity of the boat and the type of water that she will be used in are also important. Rules of thumb derived from practical observation and experience are the best guide. In general, a short boat will need to be stubbier than its longer counterpart, and so proportionally higher-sided, but this is not a given.

In kayaks, you must think about freeboard in relation to the deck peak as well as the sheerline, or you are liable to end up with too high a boat. You can alter the shape and height of either line to suit your needs. A high-decked boat with a lot of curve in the sheer can be made to have an effectively higher freeboard by making the sheer flatter, without changing her overall profile. The converse is also possible.

Rocker affects a boat's turning ability. It is important to keep the rocker generally in proportion to the length. Short boats usually have more rocker than longer ones for the same effect. In lengthening a boat you may need to redistribute the curve of the rocker without changing the actual numbers too much. In other words, in making your boat longer you may decide that the rocker of 2 inches in the keel is a good compromise, but in the original that 2 inches takes place in the 5 feet between the center of the boat and the ends. You may need to make the curve a little less steep to get the same effect if you add a couple of feet to the boat. If a short boat has a roughly equal distribution of area forward and aft of amidships, the rocker may well follow this too. If you change the distribution of sectional area, remember that you may want to change the rocker to reflect this.

Changes to a boat's sections go right to the center of things, since this seems to affect the very heart and soul of a particular boat. Bilges can be made slacker or harder.

Deadrise can be manipulated, and hollow put in or taken out of waterlines.

Sometimes this can be straightforwardly motivated, as in making an entrance sharper to cut down on pounding or adding more flare forward to retard a tendency to submarine. You might feel that a particular boat has too much bearing aft in comparison with her forward sections, and that this is making her broach when you surf in a following sea, or maybe there is an imbalance in the distribution of her wetted surface that causes the same problem.

At other times, a change in sectional change can be engendered by a more intuitive feeling that can't be pinned down as to reason, as when I made a kayak with extremely hollow ends because a little seemed to go a long way. As occasionally happens, my intuition was off, and the boat was a plunger that ran her bow under right to the cockpit rim whenever I caught a good wave, whereupon she would reach a point of equilibrium and continue on her merry way, pouring water into the cockpit unless I was wearing a spray skirt. This illustrates a good point. You can't always predict the result of a modification, and the more elemental the modification the more true this is.

It is hard to offer practical advice on sectional changes, for they are highly specific to each boat. But a few general concepts might be cautiously put forth. Deadrise can affect a boat's speed and stability as well as her bite on the water. Deadrise, the angle of the bottom planks in relation to the horizontal, is an important factor in planked canoes and kayaks because it is the element that gives them their shape, helping them approximate curved surfaces. Too much deadrise creates less wetted surface and more speed, but at a loss of stability. Too little makes for boxy, square hulls, which are quite good for capacity and stability but lack a certain thoroughbred quality. In rough water, the square chines and flat sides tend to catch on waves and spray.

Flare is an essential ingredient in making a good paddling boat, giving stability (and especially reserve buoyancy) and dryness without maximizing wetted surface. It allows for sharp ends that can still rise to oncoming seas. Too much flare will create a wide, hard-to-paddle boat that may lack initial stability if most of its volume is held as reserve buoyancy. A classic downriver racing kayak might be a good example of this type of stability/ buoyancy/wetted surface relationship.

The hardness or slackness of the bilges is another key point. In plain English, this concerns itself with the curve of the bottom, and how it looks. Does most of the curve take place at one spot, or is it distributed evenly along the whole section?

A flat-bottomed boat is an extreme example of a hard bilge, wherein the entire change in direction from horizontal to vertical (or nearly so) occurs at the single chine.

A cylinder might be the ultimate slack bilge, since it has a constant angle of change all around it. The bigger the radius, the softer the bilge.

There is unfortunately no set rule that states that a hard bilge results in one type of performance and a soft bilge gives another, which is not to say that the concept of hardening or softening a given boat's bilge may not change a characteristic such as her stability or her ease of motion in a consistent and hopefully predictable manner.

Procedures

The first work of modification takes place in the imagination, in the form of "what if's" and "what I'd like to see's." But sooner or later you are going to need to be grounded in reality. The most painless way to do this is with paper and pencil.

Rough sketches are a good starting place. One or two of my favorite designs started out as doodles on an envelope. If you have a good eye, which means if your sketches look good to you (in proportion and handsome), then you can get pretty far this way.

What I do is draw out the boat, or realize that I like the thing I've been scribbling. I might work on it, using an eraser, but a lot of times the original is pretty good since it's unfettered by desire and conscious manipulation. If I'm afraid to lose that freshness, I might trace the sketch and modify the tracing. I usually have an overall length in mind, and the sketch is automatically in scale since you draw it the way it should look; all you have to do is find out what that scale is. An architect's rule with different scales is a good way to do that. Lay it on the drawing and find the scale that most closely matches what you imagine the LOA is, and use that scale to read your heights and beams. An engineer's scale, with different decimal divisions per inch, is another excellent tool for this, especially since it deals in pure units rather than feet and inches.

If you're not comfortable working freehand, you can try using ruled graph paper. Or you can start right out in a formal drafting situation with a baseline, stations, and a known scale. This isn't such a bad idea, because you really are going to end up doing some fairly accurate drawing if you want to see what kind of boat all your changes bring about. Don't use a lot of stations at first; they just make for clutter and hard fairing. By drawing on tracing vellum you can overlay drawings and compare directly.

Another technique I've used is to loft in large scale, but not full size. For canoes and kayaks, half size is often quite feasible. I use light pencil lines and a good eraser, and make it up as I go.

Sometimes I combine this with modifying the mold and the lining out as I'm building. This has the advantage of being as close to the real thing as possible, since you are working in three dimensions. Sometimes I think this method offers a lot of freedom, and other times I find it horribly frustrating. I think it has to do with how strong a mental image I have of the boat I'm trying to create.

The basic sequence here involves doing some drawing, full or half size, to get the basic sections; these may not be completely faired, and probably aren't if I just used waterlines and sections in the drawings. I set these sections as drawn on a good strongback, a box section preferably, and begin a combination of lining out and battening off for the plank shapes. I try to use fairly square-sectioned battens because they give the best visual rendering of the plank edge (at least they do for me). What I am doing in essence is defining the plank shapes and making sure that the chines (if it is a hard-chine boat) line up in fair curves, too. Being able to see the hull full size, and to see the progression of her shape from midsection to end, is very valuable in visualizing the design's potential. If it looks as though there is too much bearing aft, or if the garboard is being asked to take an impossible twist at the stem, this is the best time to rec-

ognize the problem and remedy it. The drawback is that I need to keep cutting back the molds, or sometimes adding a strip onto a section, and rebeveling, to make it all come out fair. I need to be very careful to keep the sides of the boat symmetrical, and it is very easy to lose this. Having lots of reference lines and using a tick strip or dividers to transfer measurements seems to work well for me.

I find that the scrub plane and my fishtail gouge are the best tools for this kind of work, they being a small-boat builder's equivalent of the adze. For removing big chunks, a saber saw does a good job. Before you make them, mark all your cuts on both sides of the boat and leave the line for reference, otherwise you will get lost, and ½ inch on the starboard garboard will become ¾ inch to port. Make all the marks from keel to sheer, because once you start chopping, all references fall by the wayside.

I'm not sure if this manner of designing a boat would be acceptable to a "purist," but it is a good way to evolve something as you go along.

When it comes time to make the planks, and you don't have the security of measured drawings to fall back on, you will need to spile the planks or to use the method Tom Hill outlines in his *Ultralight Boatbuilding* book. The latter method is simple and foolproof and has a lot to recommend it, but detailed discussion of any of these methods is out of the scope of this appendix.

C. Adapting Designs for Tack and Tape

One of the great things about tack and tape is that there is no real limitation to the designs one can build in it. Dories, skiffs, hard-chine kayaks, many lapstrake boats (including canoes), and V-bottomed hulls can all be translated directly into the medium. Many round-bottomed boats, however, may need a slight rethinking to make the transition. Here are a few ideas to bear in mind.

Tack-and-tape boats shine by their simplicity. Boats specifically designed with the method in mind are kept very basic in their forms, usually being reduced to a few broad planes, and they are generally chined. There is a reason for this.

They are essentially plywood boats, and plywood is a sheet material. Without stating a hard and fast rule, it is normally better to use sheet material as sheets rather than to cut it up into narrow strips and planks. You save on labor and waste as you do this. This is not to say that you must turn any taped-seam boat into a chined design, but some move in this direction can reduce the number of planks needed, which saves you work.

Another important reason has to do with the quantity of effort, which isn't quite the same as labor. If you reduce a canoe to a four-planker or a kayak to a three-planker, the seams can be taped rather quickly and easily. If you double the number of planks the work of taping (and the materials involved) increases too, and the method is no longer as attractive. If you are interested in the subtleties that multiplank round-bottomed hulls can produce, other methods may well be more appealing to you.

Carvel-planked and glued-lap construction come to mind immediately, and I imagine that strip building and cold molding are probably worth thinking of too, although these last two are still pretty labor intensive. At some point the number of seams to be taped (and the width of the planks they represent, the minimum tape width you want to use being about 2 inches) becomes self-defeating. There are too many seams and not enough room. For me the work of making good-looking taped seams would outpace the simplicity of the method somewhere around six planks. It seems there might be easier, prettier ways to get the same hull—and with the way weight can build up with glass and resin, lighter too. But if the ease and forgiving qualities of the method attract you, test it to its limit, which may be quite different for you than for me.

Other factors enter in. Maybe you don't have a lot of clamps and don't care for their expense. You can buy a lot of glue and tape for the cost of a dozen big clamps. Maybe you feel that the method suits your level of skill and commitment. These are important reasons.

Nevertheless it is good to try to reduce the number of planks in a design if you are adapting it for taped-seam construction. It is entirely possible to do this without compromising the original design to a great extent, provided one is careful, lucky, or both.

Some study of the Wee Lassie midsection is in order. (See Figure 2-2.) This boat was originally done in six or seven planks, which is fine for riveted cedar. In glued-lap six planks is about right, since the garboard and the first broad are combined. But the Wee Lassie can easily be drawn as a taped-seam boat with only five planks, with but little loss of bearing and volume. It is even possible to draw her as a four-plank boat (Figure 2-3) and not lose the flavor of the original to any great extent. I don't think you are giving much away, hydrodynamically speaking. Perhaps a little final stability, a little resistance to pounding, and a little hull volume. It might be argued that the sharper-floored model would be a faster paddler, but I'm not prepared to comment one way or the other. My guess is that any of the versions would be a fine boat, although aesthetically the original six-to-seven plank boat probably has the sweetest lines.

Notice how the reduction in planks is accomplished. It is basically a matter of juggling the control points that define the curves, or chines in this case. A good way to do this is to draw the original in a convenient scale, and then trace over that with Mylar or vellum until you get a shape that does what you want. Having the original underneath for comparison is a great help.

The midship section is the best place to start. When you are happy with that you can do the other sections. Start by drawing the sheer, keel, and ends in profile, using the profile view of the design you are adapting. Since your boat is chined, take the chine heights from the midship section and spot them in on the profile view. What I do then is to trace the run of the planks for the hull right out into the ends, essentially eyeballing them and lining them out on paper (Figure C-1). I use the plank lines in place of waterlines as in classical drafting, but this variation is acceptable. When the plank runs look good I read the heights of the chines at the various stations and use that information to rough in either the remaining sections or a half-breadth drawing.

The only information I have is heights above the baseline, so if I choose as the next step drawing the remaining sections, I draw lines parallel to the base at the des-

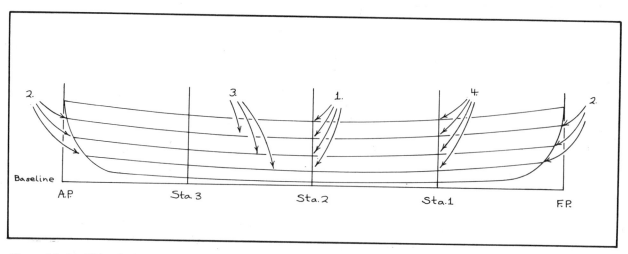

Figure C-1. Modifying for Taped Seam: Developing the Other Sections. Begin by drawing a profile with keel, sheer, and ends, using existing offsets or sketching freehand. Next, spot in chine heights (1) from the midship section you have drawn (see Figure 2-2). Determine the relative widths of the planks at the ends (2). Some upsweep in the garboard helps the planks above to run more or less parallel to the sheer. Now sweep your curves from the end points through the midship section control points (3) to make graceful, fair chine lines. Measure where these curves cross the other station lines (4). This gives the heights which can be scaled off the drawing.

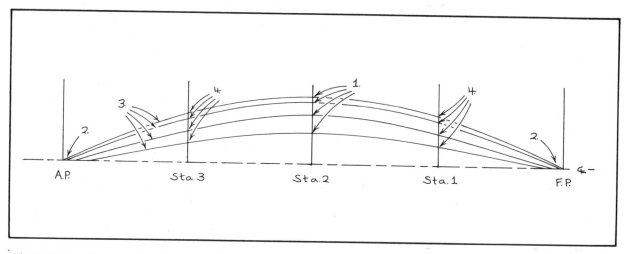

Figure C-2. Modifying for Taped Seam: Developing Half-breadths. Begin by drawing the centerline of the keel and stems. Draw the sheer from offsets or by eye. Get the end points for the planks (distance from forward or aft perpendicular) from the offsets or the profile drawing. Spot in the half-breadths of the midstation from the midship section you drew (1). Next, sweep the curves from the end points (2) through the control points (1) to make fair curves that create the type of waterline you seek. Note how the mild reverse curve in the ends creates some hollow in the fore and aft bodies (3). Finally, scale off the half-breadths for the other sections from the drawing (4).

ignated heights. I know that each half-breadth I want is somewhere on the appropriate line. I may just sketch in a section trusting my eye to make it close to what I want, and trusting it to flow into the adjoining sections in a logical manner that is close to a fair curve.

Alternatively, I may do a half-breadth drawing first (Figure C-2), and sketch the chine lines on that, treating them like classical waterlines. Or I may do a combination of both. No matter which one I do, I will have to do the other view sooner or later, and to modify that in light of the other—and so on.

What I am trying to do at first is something closer to a rough sketch than a finished drawing, something that I constantly redraw and refine to coax the control points

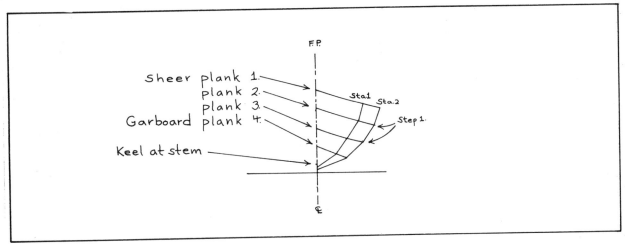

Figure C-3. Modifying for Taped Seam: Developing the Sections. Begin by setting up a baseline and centerline, using auxiliary perpendiculars to help establish heights above the base (only forebody is shown for clarity). Next, plot all points—half-breadths and heights—for each section, and connect them (1). Draw in curves across sections that indicate planks. Check your curves for fairness. If they don't look right, readjust them and transfer those adjustments to the preceding drawings.

closer and closer to defining a fair shape. If they are really close I should be able to plot the sections (Figure C-3) and draw a fair curve from bow to stern through all the points on a chine line. If the scale is large enough (1½ inches to 1 foot) I might even be pretty close. I am making *no* claim that this is how to loft; it is just a quick and dirty way to sketch up a design.

Before the design can be built it will need to be faired further, either through the conventional lofting process or by fairing on the mold. I have had some good luck with the latter option, but one or two disasters too, so you can decide for yourself how to proceed. To loft the design, you need to read the approximate offsets from your scale drawings, scale these up full size on your lofting floor or other surface, and then fair as necessary, making adjustments in control points in one view and transferring these to the other views until your battens describe fair curves.

There is a certain tension present in the process of reducing the number of planks. What is good for the builder may not be good for the design. It would be easy to cut the heart out of a design by an insensitive adaptation of the original. And the aesthetics can fly out the window too. Big, broad planks in ugly sweeps can make something that was once graceful rather hideous. For that reason it is important to draw the run of the planks

and to pay attention to their widths, tapers, and relative sizes.

When planks are too wide you also run the risk of incorporating twist or compound curvatures that a plywood sheet will refuse to take. This is a particular risk in the garboard plank (the plank nearest the keel). If your garboard is too broad, and the plywood cannot be forced into the curve it is asked to take, you can try padding out the mold edges to relieve the twist.

If you are really unsure, or want to have some low-cost fun, make a scale model of the design first. Foam-core mounting board (purchased at a framer's shop or art supply house) would make wonderful mold material, and you could plank with oaktag or something similar.

The whole process boils down to fooling around with a few variables: the widths and angles of the plank, the positions of the chine. Often the crux of the matter (at least in making a round-bottomed boat into a chined one) is in the width of the garboard and its angle of deadrise combined with the next one or two planks that make up the turn of the bilge.

It's a matter of developing a feel through experience. I am certainly not an expert; I just enjoy that kind of thing. Maybe that's half the battle. One thing is sure—if you don't like erasing, don't even start.

INDEX